CRITICAL STUDIES OF
KEY TEXTS

Charles Dickens'
Great Expectations

Nicola Bradbury

D0108062

St. Martin's Press
New York

First published in the United States of America in 1990

Printed in Great Britain

ISBN 0-312-05657-5 cloth   ISBN 0-312-05658-3 paper

Library of Congress Cataloging-in-Publication Data

Bradbury, Nicola.
    Great expectations / Nicola Bradbury.
        p.   cm. — (Critical studies of key texts)
    Includes bibliographical references and index.
        ISBN 0-312-05657-5 (cloth) — ISBN 0-312-05658-3 (pbk.)
        1. Dickens, Charles, 1812-1870. Great expectations. I. Title.
    II. Series.
    PR4560.B7 1990
    823 .8 — dc 20   90-46986
                                                               CIP

Contents

Note on the Text

Great Expectations was first published in 1861, then in a revised edition 1867–8. An authoritative modern text is expected in the Clarendon edition of Dickens's works. Since this is not yet available, I have used the helpful Penguin text edited by Angus Calder (Harmondsworth: Penguin, 1965) which includes a Note on the Text and an Appendix with the ending originally proposed by Dickens. All references are to this edition. Since, however, there are many different popular editions available, I have given references to chapters, which are short and more easily identifiable in various editions, as well as the Penguin page numbers.

Acknowledgements

I regret that the customary anonymity of publishers' readers prevents my making due acknowledgement of several helpful suggestions for the prefatory sections of this work. I also owe thanks both to many critics from whom I have learned about Dickens and to friends and colleagues who have kindly read parts of the manuscript. I am grateful to Dr Dinah Birch, Susanne Greenhalgh, Dr Clare Hanson, Dr Robyn Marsack and Dr John Pilling, and to Lionel Kelly for his encouragement.

Preface

Great Expectations is as inviting as the name implies. It also offers a challenge. How do we go about discussing a novel which is immediately accessible to all readers, which is gripping, entertaining, moving, intimate – and yet which seems more and more complex and increasingly resistant to critical analysis, the longer and the deeper we look at it? Such a novel puts criticism itself to the test, continually raising questions as to the adequacy and appropriateness of our procedures.

With these questions in mind, I have tried to do two things throughout this book – if not at once, yet as closely as possible together. My first aim is what used to be called 'critical appreciation', acknowledging and celebrating the qualities and workings of the novel. But in relation to this, I have also tried to expose and sometimes to comment on my own critical procedures and others commonly used with the novel form. Plot, structure, symbolism, scene, and particularly character are amongst the concepts explored in this way. Because *Great Expectations* is a first-person narrative, a fictional autobiography, the text promotes this kind of critical awareness or self-consciousness over both narrative and reading processes. Innocence and sophistication are built in to the tale and its telling: it is a book that works on several levels, but constantly asks us to move between them and to recognise that we are doing so.

This is an ambitious argument, since it claims to cover every aspect of this very various work – more than we can actually examine in the space available here. So this reading is designed to be provocative, and to promote discussion, rather than pre-empting all questions. Some are deliberately raised and not answered. Some characters, and some aspects of the text, are given much fuller attention than others which the reader may want to investigate further. This guide is necessarily incomplete: a prompt towards a reading of *Great Expectations*.

I

Contexts

Historical and Cultural Context

PUBLICATION

Great Expectations was published in weekly instalments in Dickens's magazine *All the Year Round* from December 1860 to August 1861.[1] Each part contained one or two chapters. There was also an issue in longer monthly numbers, nine overall; then finally the volume publication, whose three books correspond to the stages of Pip's expectations. Dickens later revised his text for the 1868 edition of his works, but most of the changes are minor (though some are noticed in our reading).

Two points are worth making about the publication of the novel. Dickens's chosen method, with relatively cheap part form followed by volume publication, allowed a wide variety of readers access to the work. And he used the technical constraints of the book's divisions as positive structural features in the novel, building plot and shaping theme around the continual fluctuations of suspense and fulfilment in the narrative. Thus the socio-economic and the structural aspects of publication are turned to account, both in developing the relations between the author and his readers, and in the themes and techniques of the novel itself.

CONTEXT: PLACING AND PERSPECTIVE

Just as the publication of *Great Expectations* both creates and expresses interesting links between the world of the novel and the world into which it came, the world of its author and readers, so we find ambivalence or duality running through the contextualisation and the intertextuality of the novel (its placing in history and in literary space), both in terms of the Victorian period and in Dickens's own career. The 'dating' of the novel, or its location in time; the link between the fictional modes of the novel and the social issues it treats; the place of the novel in Dickens's *oeuvre*: each of these aspects of the novel sets up a kind of double perspective through which it can be both seen and placed. This sense of perspective (which also runs through the text in the ironic plot, ambiguous language and ambivalent narrative stance) helps to establish a context for the intricate narrative mode of fictional autobiography.

This is a different matter from history. Instead of distance, monumentality, authority, it involves intimacy and exploration. The text is not a finished record of experience, but lives in its own present as we read. John O. Jordan ('The medium of *Great Expectations*', p. 81) explains: 'Autobiography, for Pip, means more than telling the truth about his life; it is also a way of finding out that truth.' The vitality of the text is caught between two apprehensions of experience, each incomplete: a middle-aged man's looking back to a youth looking forward. In this novel, the familiar (though still mysterious) processes of memory and anticipation realise in narrative terms what theorists today claim to be true of all texts, as Terence Cave (*Recognitions: A study in poetics*, p. 207) summarises the position derived from Roland Barthes: 'Meaning is not an essence, located in a particular place, but a function, a process always in motion towards a potential predicate or back from it through the network of anticipatory signs; recognition is the hinge on which that process turns.'

DATING: PAST AND PRESENT

This view seems extremely apt to *Great Expectations*, but it might appear to compromise any claim to historical specificity in the text. Indeed, it is true that no dates are mentioned in *Great Expectations* but the sense of period, of time, and of history both within the narrative and surrounding it are strong, and they are important to the full realisation of its themes. Dickens gives us some historical clues. Phrases such as 'for their days were long before the days of photographs' (Ch. 1, p. 35) or 'I derived from this last, that Joe's education, like Steam, was yet in its infancy' (Ch. 7, p. 76) contribute to the period feeling, and they also set up a sense of the time passed between Pip's childhood and the instant of writing. References to the characters' ages and to the passing of years also help consolidate the sense of time. We know that the story extends over some thirty years, and is set some time before 1860, when Dickens began the novel. The lapse of time in the text for Pip as child, adult, and eventually narrator is surrounded and echoed by the slightly larger space between Dickens's own childhood and this work. And both Pip's and Dickens's 'personal history' are also located within a wider social history which enables and conditions private achievements. The development of Pip and the changes in his fortunes take place at a time of change in society. Pip's social ambition to be a gentleman, locked in with Magwitch's equally social ambition to make him one, in defiance of the system which has made *him* a convict, together act as a critique for the structure and values of that Victorian world.

Robin Gilmour (*The Novel in the Victorian Age: A modern introduction*, pp. 2–4) has given a succinct account of the 'unprecedented change' in England between the start of Victoria's reign, which is where the fictional opening of Pip's story belongs – the mid-century – which would correspond to the moment of Pip's return at the end of the novel, and that later perspective from which both Pip as narrator and Dickens in writing survey those earlier developments. The doubling of the population during the first half of the nineteenth century; the startling growth of urbanisation; the social mobility financed in economic terms and realised in physical terms by the development of the national railway network; social reform in revisions of the criminal code, improvements in education and literacy, some advance in conditions of work and in provision for the destitute; political change in the challenging of an exclusive and corrupt system of parliamentary representation: all such changes contribute to the vital sense of flux, and hope of advance, from the early to the mid-century, which was then gradually transmuted into the disappointments of the materialism which succeeded that growth.

Humphry House (*The Dickens World*, p. 157) long ago pointed out that Pip's and Magwitch's aspirations are the same, for both correspond in effect to a class view and a historical and economic moment that we may take to be the author's own:

> the book is the sincere, uncritical expression of a time when the whole class-drift was upwards and there was no reason to suppose that it would ever stop being so. The social ideals of Pip and Magwitch differ only in taste.

This reading lays stress on the positive tones of the novel:

> *Great Expectations* is the perfect expression of a phase of English society: it is a statement, to be taken as it stands, of what money can do, good and bad; how it can pervert virtue, sweeten manners, open up new fields of enjoyment and suspicion. The mood of the book belongs not to the imaginary date of the plot, but to the time in which it was written; for the unquestioned assumptions that Pip can be transformed by money and the minor graces it can buy, and that the loss of one fortune can be repaired on the strength of incidental gains in voice and friends, were only possible in a country secure in its internal economy, with expanding markets abroad: this could hardly be said of England in the 'twenties and 'thirties. (p. 159)

But of course the 'upwards drift' of fortune does not go unchallenged in the novel: its treatment of money, materialism and upward mobility radically expose the 'unquestioned assumptions' of gentility. James Brown (*Dickens: Novelist in the market-place*, p. 167) argues

> One must look past his confusions and omissions, his artistic weaknesses and mistakes of historical foresight (e.g. his fear that a mid-Victorian revolution was imminent) to recognise that Dickens saw more of the tensions and contradictory social realities of industrialism underlying the stable and prosperous surface of mid-Victorian England than any other contemporary writer.

One reason Brown proposes for Dickens's percipience was his self-consciousness in the ambivalent position of a richly successful author, who was famous for his satires on *arriviste* materialism. There is both moral and psychological interest in this irony, as well as an economic and sociological perspective. In his book *Dickens, Money, and Society* (p. 174) Grahame Smith claims that Dickens's 'lasting concern is with the destructive effects of the material upon the spiritual. . . .Now we see Dickens merging the motif of money and gentility with the most intimate of human emotions, that of love.' And Taylor Stoehr (*Dickens: The dreamer's stance*, p. 102) allegorises the phenomenal world of *Great Expectations* in much the same vein: 'The conflict between the worlds of Newgate (or the Forge) and Satis House is a conflict in Pip's soul.' Such spirituality is not traduced, however, but more firmly grounded, when the historical aspects of the novel are recognised. Studies such as Alexander Welsh's *The City of Dickens* or *The Victorian Novelist: Social problems and social change* edited by Kate Flint give material from contemporary sources – factual and statistical studies of the conditions of life in the novel's contextual world – which very properly prevent our moving too readily from the specific circumstance of the text towards a more manageable, but disembodied, de-historicised version of that world as mere metaphor for the soul.

The historical context of *Great Expectations* is itself complex, and discovering more about it will help us to recognise the intricacies of the novel, both in terms of theme and the ways in which those themes are expressed, including plot, symbolism and character development, for example. Our sense of these issues as we are actually reading is further enhanced by the technique of 'back-dating' or 'ante-dating'. Writing in 1860, Dickens has his novel begin back in the time of his own childhood. This is a complex, but not unique, device: Thackeray and George Eliot were amongst many other Victorian novelists who used the technique. It brings in a further reach of time between the fictional opening of the story and the actual moment of composition (and naturally, first reading) which allows more scope to the author's, the reader's and the novel's historical sense. There is, however, a danger to set against that clarifying historical view: the risk of distortion through nostalgia. The medium of time, artfully extended by back-dating, and foregrounded by the continual movement between different 'present' moments in the text, might reveal, but might also obscure, truth. Dickens's mastery lies in the exploitation of this very danger. The integration of his authorial strategy of back-dating with the self-exploration of his central character makes for a crucial nervous tension between history and nostalgia in the narrative that exposes the workings of Pip's inner being. The interaction between past and present, the contamination and enlargement of the moment by guilt and desire, by hindsight and anticipation, by perception and recognition: these fluctuating tendencies give life to the text and the teller. *Great Expectations* can, in this sense, be read as part of the Romantic and post-Romantic development of literary exploration of the self: part of the movement from Wordsworth's poem *The Prelude* to Proust's *A la recherche du temps perdu*.

GENRE: MODE AND ISSUES

One significant difference between the time of composition of *Great Expectations* and the time when it is set lies in the fictional form itself, particularly the competition of a number of sub-genres within the 'Victorian novel', each characterised by a distinctive stylistic mode, and dealing with certain conventional themes. By 1860 domestic realism dominates the work of Thackeray, Mrs Gaskell, George Eliot, Trollope and others, and this mode contributes to the texture of *Great Expectations*, particularly as Pip begins to take an adult place in society. But there are many other fictional strains, clearly developed from earlier popular novelistic sub-genres, challenging stylistic orthodoxy with their vulgar panache. The effect of this interplay between modes, which the Russian formalist Bakhtin called 'dialogism',[2] is to unsettle the status quo, replacing 'expectations' with experimentalism in the novel.

Michael Wheeler has conveniently grouped the 'fads and fashions' of the novel form in the 1830s and 1840s in his *English*

Fiction of the Victorian Period 1830–1890. First he lists Carlyle's *Sartor Resartus* (1833–4), an enormously influential work whose themes include education, the place of the individual in society and the plight of the poor. Then comes a series of lesser achievements – yet ones which leave their trace too in *Great Expectations*. Historical novels are the first: we have already considered some of the ways in which this term shifts emphasis in relation to our work. Next, 'silver-fork' fiction, indulging snobbery and the fantasy of high-society luxury and manners. Pip's social ambition and his experiences both with Estella and with Bentley Drummle and his like in London take on a new sharpness as variants of the 'silver-fork' school. We might even surmise that Dickens makes a sly allusion to this school when Pip first arrives in London and learns from Herbert Pocket how gentlemen conduct themselves at table,

> mentioning that in London it is not the custom to put the knife in the mouth – for fear of accidents – and that while the fork is reserved for that use, it is not put further in than necessary. It is scarcely worth mentioning, only it's as well to do as other people do. Also, the spoon is not generally used over-hand, but under. This has two advantages. You get at your mouth better (which after all is the object), and you save a good deal of the attitude of opening oysters, on the part of the right elbow. (Ch. 22, p. 203)

A different extreme of romance from such gentility animates 'Newgate' novels, centred on criminals and shadowed by the gallows. This world is found, also, in Pip's experience: cheek by jowl with the silver-fork – indeed, financing it, but also overturning the fantasies of fashion. The Newgate novel is closely linked with the sensation novel, somewhere between the antique Gothic mode and Victorian melodrama, stressing the horror of darkness and death. It is through his links with Magwitch, and particularly at the convict's end that Pip's deeper feelings come to displace his pretensions to social veneer. Last in this list of popular subdivisions of the novel genre comes the suspense novel (brought to its peak by Dickens's friend Wilkie Collins in *The Woman in White*, 1859). The suspense element is the ironic pivot of plot and theme in *Great Expectations*.

Popular sub-genres of the Victorian novel are recast in this masterpiece, their energies captured but redirected. There are also further literary forms making an effect: the *Bildungsroman*, or novel of development; autobiography; the enduring structures of myth, fairy-tale and indeed tragic drama. A detailed reading is needed to detect and analyse all these mingled effects, which are both various and entertaining. Here, however, we can notice the economical and intriguing way in which Dickens has harnessed these available fictional modes to treat a wide range of apparently disparate themes on both personal and social levels: from the growing child to the gentleman; from society, money, crime, to love.

GREAT EXPECTATIONS IN DICKENS'S WORK

John Forster, Dickens's friend and biographer, reports that the author wrote to him when he began working on *Great Expectations*, giving the name and germ of the novel, and explaining that 'To be quite sure I had fallen into no unconscious repetitions, I read *David Copperfield* again the other day, and was affected by it to a degree you would hardly believe.'[3] While a survey of Victorian novelistic sub-genres alerts us to the range of situations, themes and modes used in *Great Expectations*, only a look at its place in Dickens's own career can really bring out the subtlety with which the author returns to his recurrent preoccupations but re-balances theme and treatment in this masterpiece.

Three novels offer the deepest comparisons: *Oliver Twist* (1837–9) from his early work, *David Copperfield* (1849–50) in mid-career, and *Our Mutual Friend* (1864–5) which followed *Great Expectations* and is the last complete novel by Dickens. Over this span Dickens proposes the possibility of linking Newgate sensationalism with the novel of development, tracing the career of a young boy treatened by the criminal world in discovering his identity. He deploys the first person narrator in the evolving form of fictional autobiography. And eventually he shifts the emphasis from the individual to describe the depth and perversion of social conditioning and constraints, scarcely to be confronted with the strength of personal morality, natural feelings, or individual resources.

Scanning Dickens's work barely hints at what he does. We need close reading, extensive structural analysis, time and energy to dig out all there is to be found. Early readers thought the best way to distinguish his gifts was by concentrating on characters: individuals who could be picked out for appreciation. The elements of the novel, however, of which character is only one, work together. Whatever their historical context or intertextual play, their first place is in the individual work. It is within the novel, within its world, its story, its narrative method, and in relation to its themes and all its other figures that each character is seen and understood. This articulate integrity of effect reaches its full development in *Great Expectations*. We might think of Oliver Twist asking for more, of Wilkins Micawber supping punch and waiting for something to turn up, figures rising almost clear of their contexts. But we cannot imagine Miss Havisham without her painful history, her fierce scheme for vengeance, Estella, Pip himself, and all the surrounding complications and fascinations of the novel crowding into our minds. *Great Expectations*, in the interconnections of all the characters and their stories, gives in effect the fullest development of a challenge Dickens had laid out for himself and the reader in the first sentence of *David Copperfield*: 'Whether I shall turn out to be the hero of my own life, or whether that station will be held by anybody else, these pages must show.'

Critical Reception
of the Text

The critical history of *Great Expectations* begins with Dickens's own letters to John Forster during the composition of the text, and the interchange with Bulwer Lytton which led to his recasting the ending of the novel (both are recorded in Forster's *The Life of Charles Dickens*, 1872–4). The author at work is clearly conscious both of text and context, story and readership, mode, tone and response.

Philip Collins's *Critical Heritage* volume on *Dickens* (1971) (especially pages 427–43) records immediate responses to the novel. Two stand out particularly. Edwin P. Whipple (*Atlantic Monthly*, September 1861, VIII, 380–2) perceives the twin techniques of 'stimulating and baffling the curiosity of his readers', admires the plot, and notably remarks, 'We follow the movement of a logic of passion and character, the real premises of which we detect only when we are startled by the conclusions.' This is acute. E. S. Dallas (*The Times*, 17 October 1861, 6) however gives a more confused judgement: '*Great Expectations* is not, indeed, [Dickens's] best work, but it is to be ranked among his happiest.' He notes the relationship between this novel and *Oliver Twist*, and he picks up the shift in tone as *Great Expectations* progresses, producing an interest 'still sustained, but . . . of a different kind' – yet still what he recommends is the 'simple' humour, reminiscent of 'the old *Pickwick* style'. Many critics complained at the loss of Dickens's earlier lively invention (Mrs Oliphant found *Great Expectations* 'feeble, fatigued, and colourless' in *Blackwood's Magazine*, May 1862, CXL, 574–80), but some recognised both the distinctive qualities of the novel and how they might be linked to the *oeuvre*, the method of publication and the careful construction of the work.

Revered in his lifetime, Dickens's critical reputation then declined, and it is not until about 1940 that more serious and detailed attention was given to all his works, and increasingly to the later novels.[1] There are exceptions. A. C. Swinburne in *Charles Dickens* (1913) named *Great Expectations* and *David Copperfield* 'among the highest landmarks of success ever reared for immortality', remarking on the excellence of story. G. B. Shaw, in a 1937 Foreword to the novel, asserts: 'Dickens did in fact know that *Great Expectations* was his most compactly perfect book.' What, however, Dickens did not guess, although Shaw does, is that he was 'a revolutionist': his treatment of the gentleman is in fact subversive. After this allegation it is rather surprising to find George Orwell (*Inside the Whale*, 1940) criticising Dickens's narrowness, with the assertion that 'there are large areas of the human mind that he never touches. There is no poetic feeling anywhere in his books, and no genuine tragedy, and even sexual love is almost outside his scope.'

'Modern' criticism suggests otherwise. Edmund Wilson's essay 'Dickens: The two Scrooges' in *The Wound and the Bow* (1941) explored the 'dark' Dickens and the social and moral criticism of the late novels, rather than sunny Pickwickian humour: this was enormously influential in Dickens scholarship. Humphry House (*The Dickens World*, 1941) modified the critical view of the author further by his combination of historical and imaginative attention to a cohesive Dickens world: 'a great writer is a product of the social forces of the time in which he lives, and . . . he also reflects and modifies them in his work.' John Butt and Kathleen Tillotson (*Dickens at Work*, 1957) gave scholarly attention to Dickens's working methods, showing evidence of design in novels which initial readers had supposed simple, spontaneous and chaotic. George Ford in *Dickens and his Readers: Aspects of novel criticism since 1836* (1955) heightens critical awareness further by tracing the response to Dickens's works.

These four books from the 1940s and 1950s set the foundations of subsequent Dickens criticism. Dickens's imagination is the focus of J. Hillis Miller (*Charles Dickens: The world of his novels*, 1958) who proposes that 'the Dickensian hero becomes aware of himself as guilty' – a far cry from the lament for *Pickwick*! The contextual world is delineated in many specialised studies, notably Philip Collins's *Dickens and Crime* (1962) and *Dickens and Education* (1963). The intertextual interest in literary forms pervades Robert Garis's *The Dickens Theatre: A reassessment of the novels* (1965). He describes *Great Expectations* as 'the theatrical rendering of a story which contains, deep within itself, a symbolic structure of deep imagination' (p. 206). Paul Schlicke (*Dickens and Popular Entertainment*, 1985) goes further: '*Great Expectations* is a joyously theatrical book which radically undermines the theatrical conception of character' (p. 78). Harry Stone brings in other popular forms in *Dickens and the Invisible World: Fairy tales, fantasy, and novel-making* (1980), where the conjunction of psychological concepts and archetypal patterns is well used, particularly in relation to Orlick. Taylor Stoehr (*Dickens: The dreamer's stance*, 1965) goes further into the subconscious mind and its textual enactment through premonition and recognition.

The *Dickens Studies Annual: Essays on Victorian fiction,*, vol. 11 (1983) is a *Great Expectations* issue, and includes papers picking up several of the themes mentioned here: theatrical, psychoanalytic and generic amongst them. There are also interesting discussions of Dickens in the Romantic tradition (Elliott L. Gilbert, ' "In primal sympathy": *Great Expectations* and the secret life', pp. 89–113), and of the problems of reading and writing in *Great Expectations* (Robert Tracy, 'Reading Dickens's writing', pp. 37–59; Murray Baumgarten, 'Calligraphy and code: Writing in *Great Expectations*', pp. 61–72). These last elaborate an original essay by Max Byrd called 'Reading in *Great Expectations*', pp. 259–65).

Recent critical theory has of course informed contemporary Dickens scholarship. Amongst intriguing approaches, Peter Brooks's chapter 'Repetition, repression, and return: The plotting of *Great Expectations*' in *Reading for the Plot: Design and intention in narrative* (1984, pp. 113–43) gives detailed and provocative attention to the obsessional qualities of the work.

Terence Cave in *Recognitions: A study in poetics* (1988) sets the formal structures and their associated effects in a rhetorical line stretching from Aristotle but differently interpreted by succeeding generations of readers. This usefully indicates how the focus may shift from plot to character, action to intention, and from psychology in the character to the rhetoric of response in the audience: the tissue of textuality is complex in its effects. But it is important not to be seduced into exclusive critical allegiances amongst contemporary schools if we want our attention to centre on Dickens's work. Steven Connor's brief study in Blackwell's Re-Reading Literature Series, *Charles Dickens* (1985), manages to avoid such partisanship without ignoring the insights to be gained from recent methodologies. He demonstrates a sequence of structuralist and post-structuralist approaches to selected novels, leading to a concise and suggestive Lacanian reading of *Great Expectations*. Terry Eagleton's Preface to Connor's volume charts the development of Dickens criticism as a move from realist criticism 'discovering in the novels all the prodigal richness of "life" itself' towards an aesthetic formalism which 'swaddles Dickens from history', and beyond both to work such as Connor's which 'discovers the determinations of material history in the very processes of signification of which Dickens's novels are made up' (pp. iv–v). The terminology of criticism has changed, but the impulse is still recognisable: to explore the complexities of text and to relate these to the circumstances and dynamics of its production in a way which helps us to understand our own processes of response.

Theoretical Perspectives

This reading of *Great Expectations* is not, of course, innocent of theoretical grounding or the attendant implications. We cannot shed, and therefore need to recognise, our critical experience. And that word, experience, with its ambivalent connotations, is worth noticing for it suggests both know-how, a certain ease and authority and also something quite different: the raw and surprising process by which that assurance is actually acquired. Our critical experience, then, involves a sense of innocence lost, and in this it is closely comparable with the duality of experience for Pip in the novel: the naive experience of the child, and the knowing, the explanatory, the understanding tones of the adult narrator.

If 'experience' acts as a key term in my approach, there are also several further pointers to what I have already described as 'a kind of double perspective'. Amongst these comes 'process', which I use both to describe what the novel actually does, as it unfolds, and also to indicate that these words, these strategies, these effects are working parts, devices, in the larger whole which we as readers are constructing as we go through the text, and through which we make our own imaginative version of Pip's experience. That is, the term 'process' draws attention to the active and controlled involvement in the reading of the novel by at least three parties: the author, the narrator (we could also differentiate, and add, the protagonist) and the reader.

'Dialogism' describes the function here of differing modes within the novel form, competing, clashing, keeping any single voice or tone from a dominance which might become deadening. And another frequently recurring term throughout my reading is 'subtext': that unspoken, but yet well-understood, parallel message which so often contradicts what is being openly said. Dialogism and the subtext both make rhetorical space, which in turn gives imaginative, emotional and also moral and philosphical space for 'alternative narratives' to accompany and contest the privileged version; they make room for the unspeakable, the repressed, even the unrecognised, experience.

These 'literary' aspects of the novel ought not, I think, to be separated, although they often are in critical practice, from its 'historical' qualities. My own reading, for lack of space, does not fully develop the importance of material history in *Great Expectations*. Too little is said about the conditions of life in country and city, the work done, and the particular leisure pursuits of the characters; about class distinctions – not merely between Miss Havisham and Joe, or Magwitch and Pip, but in all those nice discimations, between Mrs Joe and Biddy, for example, or Uncle Pumblechook and Mr Wopsle, or Mr and Mrs Pocket; about education, the church, the law, business and finance; about the institution of marriage. All these things, and more, need to be considered: a full reading of the novel asks us to take notice, and to make judgements based on historical materialism – even if it is often transmuted into terms which the student of literature may find more familiar, such as symbolism, description, characterisation and so on.

The importance of according due weight to history as a medium and expression of experience in this novel is not merely to claim another status for the text than myth, fairy tale, romance (while acknowledging that it has elements of all these). It is to lay stress on the fascinating and complex quality of what Pip goes through, and of what we go through in reading his narrative. The text does not give us an allegory, a coded message, something to be interpreted in secondary terms. The process of interpretation, like the processes of memory and anticipation, are part of the life of the text, part of what it is about, as well as how it works. A 'historical' reading, while it could never supersede the kind of literary procedures which take notice of the rhetoric of the novel, does, together with that textual attention, open up the workings of time itself, and our perspective on time, and hence on experience, in the novel.

This guide does not aim to prosecute or to illuminate a critical theory, but to attempt (and I hope to encourage) a reading of Dickens's novel. The work of fiction comes before the critical analysis. And my proceeding is based on the idea that this novel, in common with all others, but perhaps to a particularly marked degree, has built into it the possibility of and the clues towards a *critical* reading: an approach which takes account of the fact that we come to this work with a long history of reading, and a set of expectations about fictional texts, their workings, and the ways in which we might be expected to relate to them. The 'Great Expectations' of the title refer, in part at least, to these *readerly* expectations; Pip himself is presented as a reader, as well as the writer, of his own life; and Dickens has stressed, rather than concealed, this element of critical attention in his novel, not least through his carefully focused and complex use of Pip as both protagonist and narrator, balancing naivety and experience, youth and maturity.

Starting from the text, and looking there for directions not only in reading but towards analysis, my procedures could clearly be grouped with reader-response criticism or reception/performance theory. This approach can be briefly illustrated from Wolfgang Iser's 'The reading process: A phenomenological approach' (1972; reprinted in David Lodge's *Modern Criticism and Theory: A reader*, p. 212). Iser stresses that in considering a literary work one must notice both the text and the response to the text, for 'The convergence of text and reader brings the literary work into existence'. Iser explains the procedure by which this happens:

> As the reader uses the various perspectives offered him by the text in order to relate the patterns and the 'schematised views' to one another, he sets the work in motion, and this very process results ultimately in the awakening of responses within himself.

This 'new rhetoric' stresses the reader's conscious participation in the workings of the text. But rather than to simply support that critical school, I prefer to exploit reader-response techniques to assist in our exercise, but also to turn to other, perhaps conflicting, approaches wherever they seem potentially illuminating.

Great Expectations is a fascinating and complex novel which invites various, sometimes disparate, responses. I want to suggest such plurality through the range of critical perspectives adopted here – and also to acknowledge that yet more lines could well be followed. Historical materialism could be extended towards that kind of personal history, the biographical approach, which explores the connections between *Great Expectations* and *David Copperfield* and the records of Dickens's own early life. This involves history, of course, but also close formal analysis of Dickens's techniques of presentation, and indeed, psychoanalytical exploration of his motivation. Such an approach would look at the relationship between Magwitch's guilt and Pip's shame: the codified social morality, and the personal impulses and repressions of the psyche, in response to the forbidden. Should we label this kind of criticism historical, biographical, formal, or psycho-analytic? It is all of these things.

My point is that the pluralism of my own reading deliberately rejects strict methodological exclusivity, because I think the novel form itself challenges all such constraints. Henry James was to write in 1906 that the novel is 'more true to its character in proportion as it strains . . . its mould' (*Art of the Novel* (New York: Scribner's, 1934) p. 46). Formalist and structuralist approaches lay stress on the fable, plot, rhetorical modes and structural planning of the novel. Post-structuralism takes us further into exploring the strain between modes, the conflicting levels of interpretation and the uses (so vital here) of expectation and disappointment in the text. Adherents to any of these schools would reject the possibility of deviating from 'pure' formal analysis into interpretation: yet the post-structuralist Michel Foucault argues that form itself, the shape of discourse, is a means of expressing or repressing those kinds of power that articulate human anxiety or desire, giving play to different levels of consciousness, both individual and social, through the text. (See Michel Foucault, 'What is an author?', pp. 197–210.) Further complications in this process of expression, interpretation and inference can be gathered from the psychoanalytic theorist Jacques Lacan ('The insistence of the letter in the unconscious', p. 97):

> What one ought to say is: I am not, wherever I am the plaything of my thought; I think of what I am wherever I don't think what I am thinking.
>
> This two-faced mystery is linked to the fact that the truth can be evoked only in that dimension of alibi in which all 'realism' in creative works takes its virtue from metonymy; it is likewise linked to this other fact that we accede to meaning only through the double twist of metaphor when we have the unique key: the S and the s of the Saussurian formula [the signifier and the signified] are not on the same level, and man only deludes himself when he believes his true place is at the axis, which is nowhere.

Lacan's terminology is rebarbative, but Steven Connor has shown (in *Charles Dickens*, pp. 109–45) how his theories can be adduced in reading *Great Expectations*. The inner and outer worlds in the novel are linked through the phenomena of the imaginary and the codes of the symbolic, pre-eminently language itself: 'At the heart of Lacan's writing is a narrative concerning the psychological passage from speechlessness to language which . . . is anticipated and embodied in important ways in Dickens's works' (p. 111).

Reception theory also concentrates on language and the rhetorical organisation of the text, and it may seem appropriate to an author who loved to give public readings of his novels. It is true that Dickens did not perform his late works, but *Great Expectations* was composed immediately after an important series of public readings and it is replete with evidence of the aptitude of the text to performance (as Paul Schlicke shows in *Dickens and Popular Entertainment*, pp. 229, 246): not just a cast of recognisable and memorable characters with distinctive idioms, but a pervasive concern with levels of representation and reality, from stories to plays to ghosts and the mere memory of ideas and feelings.

Together with rhetorical, psychoanalytic and historical criticism, the fourth approach which should be listed is the feminist, where much of the liveliest contemporary work belongs. Dickens might seem a poor subject for feminist analysis: an authoritarian, exhibitionist writer whose women are notoriously liable to diminishment as child-brides, mother-substitutes, angels of the hearth, or else as ferocious harpies, dangerous to their world and particularly their families. Michael Slater's *Dickens and Women* (p. 280) gives this kind of view of Estella, and privileges Pip:

> Dickens wishes to place Pip as lover in a situation of extreme, even fantastic, hopelessness, and does not want the reader's attention deflected to the character of Estella herself. She is simply a given entity in the novel, star-like, as her name suggests, in her coldness, beauty and remote indifference to the agony and strife of human hearts. Only as a child does she seem psychologically convincing. . . . But the adult Estella must, it seems to me, be considered more as a fictive device than as a character in the mode of psychological realism.

To accept this notion would not only relegate Estella to the ranks of the 'simple', but seriously compromise the possibility of reading Pip too, as the novel invites us to do, both in and through his relationship to her and to other characters. One strength of a feminist reading lies in its willingness to rescue from obscurity certain neglected characters (not necessarily all women), and also to investigate difficult, confusing and conflicting emotions running through the text. Estella, Miss Havisham, Biddy, Estella's mother, Molly, and Pip's mother, Georgiana, and Joe's mother who is not named: all these women, and the others too, Mrs Pocket, Camilla, Clara, Miss Skiffins, would benefit from the attention of feminist criticism. Even listing these characters calls into question the view of Dickens as anathema to the feminist. That he finds room, gives voice, even accords the dignity of absence (as with those lost mothers) to these women would suggest that Dickens is not bounded by the narrowness of embattled masculinity. English and American feminism, concerned with political ideology, sociological contextualisation, the woman's experience, would find material for study in *Great Expectations*. But so would the French philosophical and formalist feminists and those interest in psychoanalysis.

The focus for these disparate, but interconnecting, lines of enquiry can be given in one word: Orlick. Taylor Stoehr (*Dickens: The dreamer's stance*, p. 127) summarises the difficulty of Orlick: 'One has the feeling that Orlick got into *Great Expectations* in spite of Dickens. . . . His minor place in the action is out of all proportion to the fearful power with which he is delineated.' And Robert Garis (*The Dickens Theatre: A reassessment of the novels*, p. 218) offers an explanation: 'We can now define Orlick as the embodiment of pure and uninhibited libido.' But Orlick is more than a sport of the psyche, an index of the unspeakable. He is related, either by plot or (more frequently) theme, to many other characters: Mrs Joe (most obviously), but also Biddy; Bentley Drummle, and all the other wife-beaters, but also, by extension, the wives, Estella, Molly; most disturbingly, he is related both arbitrarily and inevitably to Pip. In Orlick, more fiercely than elsewhere, but not really differently, there surfaces in the novel the dark side of Pip's gentlemanly and romantic ambitions and desires.

In this connection, Kate Flint's *Dickens* (p. 129) offers several significant insights, for she moves from recognising 'the presence, sometimes repressed, often marshalled, of female sexuality within the text which threatens with potentially disruptive energies' to male desire, which is 'not so obvious in the passions which motivate Dickens's heroes and villains' as in something more covert: 'the implicit creation, in terms of point of view, of a particular bond between narrator and male reader'. Kate Flint is describing Dickens's novels in general, here, but her caution is peculiarly apt to *Great Expectations* where despite the apparently seamless bond between narrator and reader, moving through the shared experience of the text towards complicity in judgement (or, more sympathetically, shared understanding), our reading will hint from time to time at disruptions in this process, fissures which expose even the mature Pip to our attention. Kate Flint implies that this kind of discrimination may come easier to the woman reader, because 'now as then, [she] is forced to insert herself into the texts and take up a positon which is not articulated through the apparent author–reader relationship.'

The acknowledgement of the hidden, the conflicting, the confusing, the celebration of 'polyphony' (or many voices), and the capacity to enjoy the subversion of order: these are all strengths of feminism that work well with *Great Expectations*, despite its masculine author, male protagonist, and 'phallocentric' society.

The novel hints at all the things which that order distorts, represses, or sacrifices, and at the human cost of such proceeding. In my own reading I have explored some of the ways in which this works with Mrs Joe, Miss Havisham and Estella, but of course this could be extended. We could consider, for example, the implicit commentary (occasionally surfacing in strikingly articulate criticism) on Pip's values, his desires, his whole mode of engagement with experience, which is offered by Biddy's patient, quiet, loving adaptability. Or, at another extreme, we might interrogate the unease of Pip's response to the scene in which Jaggers displays his housekeeper at the Gerrard Street dinner-party for the young bloods whom he holds, for the most part, in casual contempt.

> 'I'll show you a wrist,' repeated Mr Jaggers, with an immovable determination to show it. 'Molly, let them see your wrist.'
>
> 'Master,' she again murmured. 'Please!'
>
> 'Molly,' said Mr Jaggers, not looking at her, but obstinately looking at the opposite side of the room, 'let them see *both* your wrists. Show them. Come!'
>
> He took his hand from hers, and turned that wrist up on the table. She brought her other hand from behind her, and held the two out side by side. The last wrist was much disfigured – deeply scarred and scarred across and across. When she held her hands out, she took her eyes from Mr Jaggers, and turned them watchfully on every one of the rest of us in succession.
>
> 'There's power here,' said Mr Jaggers, coolly tracing out the sinews with his forefinger. 'Very few men have the power of wrist that this woman has.' (Ch. 26, pp. 236–7)

Surely this is a scene that articulates, in word, in gesture, above all in looks, a critique of male hegemony, but also of female violence, dangerous even in repression (those scars betray attempted suicide). Social dominance in the master-servant relationship underlines sexual politics. But what seems to be most interesting is that the watchful looks of both antagonists here (both pointedly looking *away*) bear an unstated relationship to the gaze of the narrator, not merely as a guilty spectator, but as he will later 'trace out the sinews' of what he sees here, when he uses this glimpse of Molly's hands to recognise the kinship between this unhappy woman and Estella.

Even the briefest examination of a moment from *Great Expectations* reveals how subtle and flexible we need to be in our reading. Taking my cue from the novel, I have used a variety of critical approaches, hoping to expose both the disparity and the integration of distinct levels of interest in the text, from narrative to imaginative, moral to social. Underlying all these is the correspondence between a procedure within the text itself and one in our reception of the text: the balance between activity and passivity, or curiosity and wonder, in our reading, meeting with the conjunction of memory and desire in Pip, and all the complexities of the first-person narrative mode. There are many phrases in the novel which seem to point out these sympathetic paradoxes. I have chosen for the key to this reading the words 'wonderful inconsistency' which Pip uses of the attitude of love, overcoming judgement, but not denying it. That inconsistency, rather than the reverse, should evoke wonder, puts criticism in its proper place in relation to the fictional text.

This reading is, I hope, suggestive and provocative. It is not, however, exhaustive, rigorously coherent, or conclusive. Although written as a single continuous discussion of the experience of reading the novel, it is presented in sections, so that a reader may find focal points for arguments of his or her own. Five sections investigate the tensions or paradoxes of the novel under divided titles, designed to promote that sense of the 'double perspective', both seeing and placing, with which I opened this introduction to the reading.

'Story/Secret' begins with an account of the novel's plot, but shows how the ironic shadowing of one action by another hidden design, emerging with the return of Magwitch, articulates the tension in *Great Expectations* in terms of story. This section also outlines the dialogism of *Great Expectations*, both in disparate modes or genres, such as fairy-tale, melodrama, grotesque, and in the competition of embedded texts within the novel.

The organisation of the work is the focus of the next section, on 'Structure/Suspense'. This opens with the publishing process itself, but moves on to show how Dickens exploited this mechanism to enhance the age-old contract between story-teller and audience for the narrative to be at once given and witheld, so that interest, and expectations, are excited as well as satisifed. This section describes the general structure of the novel, and then looks closely at two passages to show in detail how Dickens paces and controls the narrative process. There is then room to consider the use of stories within *Great Expectations* that can be read as analogues for Pip's, both contributing to and also competing with the central fable.

From structure we move to 'Scene/Subtext': dramatic moments, rather than embedded narratives, which work in comparable ways to extend and vary the development of the text. Two series of scenes are chosen as examples of two quite different tones in the text: the violent, enacted in the fight scenes, and the comic and satirical, performed by Trabb's boy.

Another kind of patterning is discussed in the section on 'Symbols/Signals' which investigates both the naturalism and the deliberate, cryptic arbitrariness of Dickens's use of imagery, symbolism, language play, names, questions, lies, fictions, ghosts and visions: in other words, the whole range of signs and symbols within the text, and something of the imaginative fluency, interrupted and made visible by the hesitancies of comic misapprehension with which this range of expressive devices is deployed.

'Character' is the subject of the next section, and the aim here is not merely appreciation but careful analysis of the various means by which Dickens constitutes the shifting, 'living' reality of Pip in relation to the other characters in the novel and the implications of this process not merely in narrative, but also psychological, and even philosophical, terms. Because this book is not a description of *Great Expectations*, but a critical guide, no attempt is made to cover every character. What I do is try to work out how it is that we could do this: what is the structure, what are the processes of characterisation in the novel and what this means for the reader. Looking at Mrs Joe, Miss Havisham, Estella, and Pip himself in relation to each other, I suggest that *Great Expectations*, while working with characters and investigating character itself, also moves beyond the limitations of idiosyncratic personality, towards a sense of what we might better call 'humanity'.

Finally, there comes a long section called 'Reading the novel' which attempts to integrate the observations and techniques of this work in an extended reading of the pivotal Chapter 39 of *Great Expectations*, placed in the context of two proleptic chapters (27 and 38) and also in relation to the subsequent movement of the novel away from 'Expectations' to acceptance, and eventually to the quiet of the conclusion. This, of course, is examined together with the rejected ending, which lives on in our critical minds as a perpetual parallel; but I find both possibilities, the open and the closed ending, held in suspension in the ambiguities of the published text.

Through this critical procedure, circling through the text, moving repeatedly over certain scenes, approached in different ways, and coming back to central problems and preoccupations in different contexts, my reading deliberately destabilises any pretence to critical control in favour of promoting the sudden fascinations and shifts of interest that I find characteristic of the experience of the text. *Great Expectations* invites and rewards, but also disappoints, our old readerly anticipations. It offers characters, story, themes, symbols, but through its subtleties it also diverts our attention from such elements of the novel towards the strange flexibilities of creation and recall, memory and desire, and the way such forces remake experience itself.

II

*Great Expectations:
A Reading of the Text*

1

Story/Secret

Charles Dickens began *Great Expectations* with the title, and he knew immediately that it was a good one.[1] Inviting our trust, as well as announcing the hero's confidence, this title turns precisely on the deepest and most complex ironies of the novel, which pursues familiar dreams only to expose their emptiness, and thwarts 'expectations' with a neat reversal which requires us to read back into the past before permitting a very different kind of progress.

The story is simple, but it is not single: its secret power lies in two crossed lines, which seem to meet by chance, but then through increasing coincidence reveal a design in which every character, every embedded narrative, every symbol of the novel is implicated. Gradually Pip's world becomes Dickens's exposition of his own society and a model of the perennial tension between individual and social man, between order and desire.

The novel follows the fortunes of Pip from the 'small bundle of shivers' at the opening, orphaned, in a graveyard (the first, most universal hint that for every future 'expectation' there is a rooted past), to the 34-year-old man of the conclusion, standing in the 'cleared space' of his memories with the last of his 'poor dreams'. This is the progress of the *Bildungsroman*, or novel of development; but it is also a familiar pattern in myth and fairy-tale and Dickens makes oblique and direct references to several such fictions, surrounding his commonplace protagonist with the aura of inherited and traditional dreams, and showing as those ambitions fail how much of the individual man is left behind.

Pip is startled in the churchyard by 'a fearful man, all in coarse grey, with a great iron on his leg' (Ch. 1, p. 36), who demands a file and food. The child steals them from the forge where he lives; but the convict is recaptured, struggling with another escaped prisoner. Pip, his secret safe, is carried home by Joe Gargery, his sister's husband and his protector.

The next great event in Pip's life is a summons to 'go and play' (Ch. 7, p. 81) at Satis House for Miss Havisham, 'an immensely rich and grim lady' (*ibid.*) who lives in secluded desolation, embalming a broken heart in her permanently darkened room. She introduces Pip to her ward Estella 'who was very pretty and seemed very proud' (Ch. 8, p. 85). He loses his heart, and learns to despise his humble origins. After a series of visits, however, Pip is abruptly dismissed with a premium of £25 to be apprenticed blacksmith, returning discontented to his old life and expectations.

It is at this time that Mrs Joe is attacked by an unknown assailant, and paralysed. Pip suspects the moody journeyman, Orlick, but what disturbs him is that the weapon used was his old convict's leg-iron and he feels obscurely responsible for the outrage. Nevertheless, he decides not to 'dissolve that spell' (Ch. 16, p. 148) of secrecy. The forge returns to order, with Pip's first teacher, the young Biddy, called in to keep house, and Mrs Joe signalling appeasement to Orlick. Pip, however, remains unsettled, and tries to 'improve himself' through study.

In the fourth year of his apprenticeship, Pip is confronted by a gentleman he recognises as Miss Havisham's lawyer. Mr Jaggers announces that he has come to release Pip from his indentures and take him to London to become a gentleman. He acts for a 'liberal benefactor' whose name must remain secret. Gladly, Pip leaves home for London and a new life.

The second stage of Pip's expectations is based in the metropolis and follows him 'educating for a gentleman' as Estella is for a lady. Amidst extravagance and folly he sustains one firm friendship with Herbert Pocket, whom he first met by chance at Satis House. Fortune strains his fellowship with Joe, however, and when Joe calls, Pip confesses, 'if I could have kept him away by paying money, I certainly would have paid money' (Ch. 27, p. 240). Joe carries a welcome summons to Satis House, and Pip has the grace to feel ashamed, though not enough to return Joe's visit when he answers Miss Havisham's call. She encourages him to escort Estella to London, and Pip supposes that his 'expectations' are to include a wife as well as riches.

This dream is destroyed when another visitor appears in Pip's rooms and reveals himself as Magwitch, the convict of the marshes. He tells Pip that he is the one who has made him a gentleman. All Pip's suppositions (and ours) have been unfounded; his whole history must be revised, and his future, moreover, adjusted accordingly – for Pip cannot now accept the convict's money.

The third stage of the novel traces a profound change. Pip must renounce his hope of Estella, his assumption of superiority and his expectation of success, revising all his values. Setting aside all self-interest, he tries to provide for Herbert, and to protect Magwitch, whose return to England is a capital offence. After clarifying his true relations with Miss Havisham, and forgiving her cruel use of his mistake, he returns to find her 'consuming' in flames, her old pretences destroyed; and he saves her at the cost of injury. He plans to spirit Magwitch abroad, but is secretly called away. Orlick, it appears, knows Pip's movements; he declares his enmity and threatens to kill him. Pip is rescued, but cannot do more than watch as his bid to escape with the convict is foiled. It is the second prisoner from the marshes – coincidentally, the man who wronged Miss Havisham – who now prevents Magwitch from evading capture. The pursuer dies, Magwitch is half-drowned, captured, sentenced and dies in prison. Pip, meanwhile, has traced the origins of Estella and found that she is the daughter of his benefactor: so, finally, though not happily, the two strands of the plot are most firmly knit together.

After the death of Magwitch, Pip suffers a grave illness; he is nursed by Joe. He thinks of returning to claim Biddy, but finds her married, the new Mrs Gargery. Now he, like Magwitch, goes abroad, to leave his old life behind, and work. Returning, he finds a young Pip at the forge, and a vivid sense of his past dreams. At Satis House he finds only ruins, but amongst them stands Estella. Her unhappy marriage has softened her and she greets him kindly. They speak of parting, but at the close it remains uncertain whether their future will be alone or together.

The bare outlines of Pip's story seem strangely familiar. An orphan, terrified by a wild man, summoned by a fairy godmother, bewitched by an icy maiden; a poor boy who goes to London to become a gentleman; a young man mysteriously raised up and suddenly humbled again: it is the stuff of fairy- and folk-tale, myth and well-known fictions. It is so because these happenings, inexplicable, arbitrary, catastrophic, correspond to the patterns of our common hopes and fears: the dream of love and riches, and the dread of loss. Both triumph and disaster arrive like a bolt from the blue – and yet they answer covert anticipations. The irony of *Great Expectations* hangs between them. Dickens heightens both the fantastic, extraordinary quality of the tale and the curious sense of recognition: the known and the unknown. The resonance of Pip's fortunes, our sense of what they represent, is amplified by echoes, both within and beyond his story. The correspondences within the fiction are complex: we can consider them later in the context of structure and of character. The extratextual references might appear more obvious: but they are surprisingly varied both in tone and function.

Dickens uses both literary fictions and non-literary texts amongst the 'resonators' for Pip's story. Every reference in the novel has some bearing on him, however oblique, and the use of these clues is to illuminate different facets of the central situation. Take the blacksmith's song, *Old Clem* (Ch. 12, p. 123), and the comic song Pip learns from Biddy (Ch. 15, p. 136). The first links 'the measure of beating upon iron' with the fire, 'Roaring dryer, soaring higher'. Pip learns it at the forge, but sings it to Miss Havisham: the woman he will eventually snatch from the flames which symbolise her destructive passions. Biddy's song, on the other hand, touches on another preoccupation of Pip's life, and ironically foreshadows his fortunes:

> When I went to Lunnon town sirs,
> Too rul loo rul
> Too rul loo rul
> Wasn't I done very brown sirs?
> Too rul loo rul
> Too rul loo rul

Pip learns the words, but he misses the message.

Biddy's first teaching text (Chapter 10) is equally significant: it is a catalogue of prices. Then there is the tract handed to Pip when (Chapter 13) he is taken to be 'bound apprentice' to Joe; this is illustrated 'with a woodcut of a malevolent young man fitted up with a perfect sausage-shop of fetters, and entitled, TO BE READ IN MY CELL' (Ch. 13, p. 132). This pamphlet answers to Pip's reluctance to be committed to Joe's calling, and to his guilt at this unwillingness. But it also recalls those first, real fetters of the convict on the marsh – and it fits, too, the metaphorical image Pip finds for the significance of his first visit to Satis House: 'the long chain of iron or gold, of thorns or flowers, that would never have bound you, but for the formation of the first link on one memorable day' (Ch. 9, p. 101).

Even a blatant text may signal a complex message. Pip listens to the 'affecting tragedy of George Barnwell' (an apprentice who murders his uncle, spurred on by his mistress) and protests: 'What stung me, was the identification of the whole affair with my unoffending self' (Ch. 15, p. 145). But that very evening he returns to find his sister laid low 'by a tremendous blow on the back of the head, dealt by some unknown hand' (Ch. 15, p. 145), and he feels dreadfully guilty: 'With my head full of George Barnwell, I was at first disposed to believe that *I* must have had some hand in the attack' (Ch. 16, p. 147). Then, when Jaggers comes to announce Pip's fortune, he finds him in the pub (Ch. 18, p. 160), once again listening to Mr Wopsle, the clerk at church and aspiring Thespian, 'imbrued in blood to the eyebrows', dramatising a newspaper account of a sensational murder trial. The scene recalls that earlier performance, and helps knit different plot strands together in relation to Pip's inner development – not just his worldly fortunes. Here the taste of criminality is more apt than Pip knows and the precipitate verdict of the 'cozy' drinkers, which Jaggers criticises, underscores the irony. Though 'George Barnwell' and the newspaper murder look like sensationalist diversions in the text, remote from Pip's own development, a suspicion grows that they have some bearing on his story. It is in recognition of guilt and innocence that Pip will eventually have to come to terms with the sudden shifts of fortune: the riches and the destitution that come from his contact with the convict.

Wopsle, for all his clownish affectation, figures in the most subtle and far-reaching of Dickens's textual resonances in *Great Expectations*: the allusion to *Hamlet*. The acme of an actor's ambition, this tragedy marks Wopsle's (alias Waldengarver's) London debut: though his 'reading' turns it into broad farce. The allusion is thus doubly removed from Pip, who is in the audience: indeed, it is heavily disguised. Nevertheless, the Ghost of the play reminds us of the many 'ghosts' half-glimpsed by Pip throughout the text; and the play itself offers a dark, inverted shadow of his story. Pip's 'adoptive father' influences him through his expectations as inescapably as a ghostly King Hamlet. Magwitch too rose suddenly amidst the graves, and he will also (like the Dane) appear unexpectedly again. His benevolence to Pip is not undiluted generosity: it is also his own revenge on the state which has sent him down under. The *Hamlet* allusion draws attention to the ambivalence of Magwitch's motives, which fuse selfishness and gratitude, and of Pip's response to him, veering between abhorrence and sympathy.

The complexity of relations between Pip and Magwitch leads to a disturbingly convoluted analogy in Pip's mind with *Frankenstein*. While Magwitch watches his protégé 'with the air of an Exhibitor', Pip compares himself with Mary Shelley's unhappy scientist:

> The imaginary student pursued by the misshapen creature he had impiously made, was not more wretched than I, pursued by the creature who had made me, and recoiling from him with a strong repulsion, the more he admired me and the fonder he was of me. (Ch. 40, p. 354)

The analogy reverses the position of creator and creature, emphasising an ambivalence of influence already suggested in the original myth. Which is the monster here? Have they not, indeed, inadvertently perhaps, made each other what they now are?

From Biddy's price list and 'Old Clem' to the George Barnwell story, *Hamlet* to *Frankenstein*, the incidental texts adduced in

Great Expectations lie lightly alongside Pip's narrative, and yet they bear quite a weight of significance. In their oblique way, uninsistent even when the texts themselves are rhetorically melodramatic, they draw attention to the underlying values and dangers of the adult world of the novel. Here, learning is linked with wealth and deception, ambition with violence, obsessional will with revenge, 'doubling' of the self and distorted creation. Even while Pip misses such signals, the reader may be alerted to the overtones of his adventure.

The story outline for *Great Expectations* is riddled with ambiguities. It seems simple, yet turns out to be complex. Failure is substituted for success, guilt for triumph, and yet this 'fall' is then redeemed. Pip's story recalls ancient patterns of wishing and disappointment; it is not made too easy for us to judge, and it turns from comedy to the reverse, and flirts with sensationalism, science fiction and the supernatural, starting from its base in realism. Most intriguing of all, the story exploits and challenges the process of story-telling itself. Against 'telling', revelation, this story sets secrecy. *Not* telling is the pivot of the plot. This is the more remarkable since the story is told in retrospect by its central character, Pip himself. Revelation and suppression are equally weighted for this narrator: and thus the narrative process itself gives us something of this complexity, the challenge, the complicity, the interest, of autobiography.

2

Structure/Suspense

Revelation competes with secrecy to control the structure of *Great Expectations*. The novel was first published in weekly parts, each containing just one or two chapters. The next division was in nine monthly numbers. Finally the book came out in three volumes: one for each stage of Pip's expectations. So Dickens turned publishing constrictions into structural resources. He used each unit (from sentence and paragraph to chapter and part, number or volume) to measure out the narrative, not as a flow, but a discrete series of anticipations and disappointments, expectations and recognitions – each one, even the last, vitally incomplete. The age-old, informal contract between story-teller and audience for attention to be rewarded with interest is highly organised. Through this technique Dickens refines the processes of narrative so that they not only give the pleasures of suspense, surprise, or gratified expectation, but act as a structural counterpart to the very experiences Pip is undergoing within the narrative. Furthermore, this effect of replication is amplified within the novel by two means: the first person narration, and the inclusion together with Pip's central story of a whole series of subordinate narratives which both feed into and reflect on his: the story of Joe, of Biddy, of Estella, of Herbert, of Miss Havisham, for example, and of course the story of Magwitch.

Narrative technique, narrative structure and the narrative line itself therefore interlock in *Great Expectations* in the treatment of the 'expectation' theme. The title encourages us to look forward; the narrator is looking back: there is a possibility of fantasy, a risk of mere historical report – but between them, the shifting, fascinating processes of exploration, corresponding to imagination, memory and reflection.

We can approach this subtlety step by step. Looking first at the units of composition, then analysing the structural features of the narrative line, and finally considering the counterpoint of single and multiple focus of narratives, we can deconstruct the shape and measure the pacing of the novel.

Three volumes form the principal structure of *Great Expectations*, distinguishing the stages of longing (Chapters 1 to 19), the 'gay fiction' of enjoyment (Chapters 20 to 39) and disillusionment (Chapters 40 to 59). These phases are punctuated by the two great narrative surprises: the bequest, and the revelation of the benefactor. Ironically, these events, which strike Pip with astonishment, are seen on reflection to form an inseparable pair. They are, moreover, part of a sequence which begins with the very first page of the novel, when Magwitch appears, and continues to the last page when his daughter Estella is brought together with Pip. So the dramatic 'peripeteia' and 'catastrophe' (the sudden turn and subversion of order) do not, after all, interrupt, but they constitute the narrative flow. It is a story moving through anticipation and disappointment to recognition.[2] Self-recognition, indeed, for it is Pip's self-knowledge which depends on his stopping to review his own story and see that it is not what he thought it was, but a different kind, with different principal characters, a different plot and a very different tone. He has to shift his point of view, and 're-read' his life.

Suspense develops from a negative device in this process towards a metaphysical condition: the 'negative capability' which Keats described as a function of genius, 'that is when man is capable of being in uncertainties, Mysteries, doubts, without any irritable reaching after fact & reason' (letter to George and Tom Keats, 21 December 1817). When Pip is promised a fortune, secrecy is imposed upon him against the itch of his curiosity; when the benefactor is revealed, he learns a deeper mystery, and comes to accept it. Dickens conducts us through suspense, which has an end, into wonder, which may be endless: the first is embroiled with worldliness, but the second shifts to a different scale of values. Suspense relies on expectation; but wonder comes, paradoxically, out of disappointment. The movement between them, back and forth, is a constant tension throughout the novel and it operates in every unit of the structure, from the whole, or the volume, to the individual chapter, paragraph, or sentence. Pip's stance, and ours, is never securely fixed.

Dickens's control, however, is secure. He not only sustains excitement through significant incidents, but with remarkable economy he makes good use of the intervening passages: pages which might seem unimportant. A fine example comes in Chapters 6 and 7: the two chapters which formed the fourth weekly part of the novel when it was first published and concluded the first 'number' in the monthly issue. These chapters have the tricky function of easing the novel from the vital first incident with Magwitch on the marshes into the 'second subject', when Pip is summoned to Satis House. How is Dickens to make this transition, without losing the interest of the audience, and yet avoid violating the secret parallel between the 'two openings', and between Magwitch and Miss Havisham, on which Pip's misconception, and the whole course of the novel, is to depend?

The answer is distance, of tone and subject matter, disguising thematic relevance. The transitional passage, a single publishing unit, is divided into two chapters. The first (6) is short, retrospective, rather serious. The second (7) is lengthy, wandering, often comical. Both seem to pause, relax from the concentration of 'great expectations'. The narrative scarcely advances, the pressure is released. Yet in this lull that aspect of Pip's story which has less to do with his fortunes than his personal development has space to grow. The issues of moral cowardice and responsibility are conjoined in Chapter 6 when Pip wonders whether to tell Joe his guilty secret. He decides not to, for fear of losing Joe's confidence. This concealment is, of course, a precondition of the novel's story. But the preternaturally adult language in which it is recorded, the abstraction and ethical weighting, act as clues to the importance of this decision on a thematic level, distinct from the plot. If we pick up these clues, then even the apparent simplicity of the last sentence in this chapter begins to seem disingenuous. We hear a warning. These matters are not to be forgotten even if the story turns away from them for a while: 'My state of mind, as I have described it, began before I was up in the morning, and lasted long after the subject had died out, and had ceased to be mentioned saving on exceptional occasions' (Ch. 6, p. 73).

Pip's confession is one of a long series of clues, narrative and stylistic, that – together with his story as it appeared to the characters surrounding him, or even to Pip himself at the time – another, hidden text is unfolding: the ironic, comical, pathetic and significant narrative which is available now to the grown man, and which may become open to us, if we read with full awareness.

This 'subtext' is what provides the rationale for Chapter 7. What looks on the surface like slack composition, wandering from Pip's early lesson to the story of Joe's childhood and then back to Pip and the summons to Satis House, works obliquely towards demonstrating the central development of the novel. The Satis House adventure at the end of the chapter will be a learning experience, just as much as Pip's first letters which begin it. Between them, Joe's history of childhood neglect, quarrelling parents, violence and tyrannical possessiveness, with his patient, loving and selfless response, does more than explain his character and Pip's background, or Mrs Joe's situation. It also stands for comparison with Magwitch's history, and Estella's, Miss Havisham's, Pip's own. So we are nudged towards a process of interpretation in the course of the chapter, when the young Pip, consoling Joe for Mrs Joe's grim appearance, 'sagaciously observed, if it didn't signify to him, to whom did it signify?' (Ch. 7, p. 78). In fact, all appearances in this world are significant – if not always in the way they first seem – and all significance is general: it is a system of expression which unites people in understanding, and divides them only when it is misconceived. The importance of Joe's example is recognised in Chapter 7, though it is so soon to be forgotten, and only much later fully appreciated. Pip as a child

> dated a new admiration of Joe from that night. We were equals afterwards, as we had been before; but afterwards at quiet times when I sat looking at Joe and thinking about him, I had a new sensation of feeling conscious that I was looking up to Joe in my heart. (Ch. 7, p. 80)

A different example of structural pacing comes in Chapter 47.

The opening of the eighth monthly number, at the middle of volume three, is not apparently an important position. Pip is here marking time, waiting for the moment to escape with Magwitch. He has lost all hope of Estella: 'an impression settled heavily on me that she was married', though he avoids discovering whether this is true. Pip's despondency fits both this emotional impasse and the enforced inactivity with Magwitch. It is appropriate to the suspended plot; but such gloom inevitably jeopardises the narrative excitement which an author-in-series can never afford to abandon. How does Dickens satisfy these contradictory requirements: to have the novel slow to a pause, and yet urge the reader on?

The chapter begins with Pip's helpless mood, the emotional counterpart to suspended action. To vary the monotony, Pip decides to go to the play before returning to bed. What he sees is a musical comedy followed by 'the last new grand Christmas pantomine': a spectacle calculated to introduce variety. It is an opportunity Dickens willingly exploits for a ludicrous interlude. The hapless Wopsle has sunk from Hamlet to this! His former pretensions are not without significance, however, for just as once the black-stockinged figure encountered his 'royal phantom' (Ch. 31, p. 274), so now 'Mr Wopsle with red worsted legs under a highly magnified phosphoric countenance and a shock of red curtain-fringe for his hair' (Ch. 47, p. 397) sees a ghost. This revenant is not on stage, however, but in the audience, sitting immediately behind the unconscious Pip. It is the very incarnation of Pip's secret anxieties, both about the past and the haunted present: Magwitch's enemy, Compeyson.

This incident is the height of melodrama, the furthest stretch of coincidence, yet in the telling, Dickens stresses, rather than conceals, these outrages to probability. As with the first appearance of Magwitch, or the first glimpse of Compeyson himself, it is this quality of assault which is most vital – for it is this which violates the safe discrimination of dreams or nightmares from waking reality, and intrudes the most fearful threat: one which half seems to come from inside.

Pip's response is not hysterical. On the contrary, his controlled disquiet, mirrored in complex and balanced sentence rhythms circling around repeated words and phrases, opposes reason against horror:

> I cannot exaggerate the enhanced disquiet into which this conversation threw me, or the special and peculiar terror I felt at Compeyson's having been behind me 'like a ghost'. For, if he had even been out of my thoughts for a few moments together since the hiding had begun, it was in those very moments when he was closest to me; and to think that I should be so unconscious and off my guard after all my care, was as if I had shut an avenue of a hundred doors to keep him out, and then had found him at my elbow. I could not doubt either that he was there, because I was there, and that however slight an appearance of danger there might be about us, danger was always near and active. (Ch. 47, p. 399)

There is a fine ambiguity in 'I could not doubt . . . that he was there, because I was there' ('I could not doubt . . . because', or, 'he was there, because'): doubt and certainty turn on the differing logic of the conscious and subconscious mind, laying bare the lines of the story. The contamination of Pip's calculation by nagging fear is a reluctant 'chill'. So Dickens harnesses the imaginative force of an almost surreal incident to the central movement of the text, making it a matter not of action but reaction, a drama of response. With this inward movement we are taken back, like Pip: we are reminded of the 'young man' on the marshes; reminded of Miss Havisham's betrayal; alerted to the present threat both to Magwitch and to Pip himself.

As Chapter 47 closes, Pip resolves to be 'very cautious indeed'. The comic interlude intended to divert the ennui of the opening has been subverted into melodrama, but this too has shifted, back into the dynamic development of the narrative – against our expectations.

Anticipation, peripeteia and disappointment are consistent features of narrative structural control throughout *Great Expectations*, although our two extracts (part four and part twenty-nine) show that they may operate in both directions: to satisfy or to stimulate the reader's expectations, but always to shift towards a new accommodation. The unitary method of composition, in chapters, parts and volumes, looks simple and cumulative, but the effects are varied through an interplay of recognition and surprise. This complex construction is further enriched by the counterpoint of distinct but related narratives, as Pip's story is interrupted and supported by what we learn of those around him.

These interpolations contribute structurally as well as thematically to the novel, since we meet and accommodate them with those very responses of surprise and recognition which distinguish our reading of Pip's story. They come, of course, in sequence – the fundamental structure of all texts – but we can consider them also, as we do in reading, according to theme, mode, or tone. So we find a series of stories about the neglected child, for example, which contextualise Pip's central fable; each one is different, not just in the main character, but in presentation. Joe's history (Chapter 7) and Magwitch's (Chapter 42) both start with a suffering child, but they take divergent lines, since Joe's is the story of patience and goodness while Magwitch moves through crime towards his death in jail. Good and bad, however, are held together (despite the distance that separates them in the text) by certain features of narration. Both are told in the first person, and both are told to Pip (though on the second occasion Herbert is present too). While the content is different, the style is rather similar, marked by short declarative sentences, repetition as a device of emphasis and coherence, and a curiously dispassionate, almost comical, sense of irony. Thus Joe's introductory summary:

> I'll tell you. My father, Pip, he were given to drink, and when he were overtook with drink, he hammered away at my mother, most onmerciful. It were a'most the only hammering he did, indeed, 'xcepting at myself. And he hammered at me with a wigour only to be equalled by the wigour with which he didn't hammer at his anvil. – You're a listening and understanding, Pip? (Ch. 7, p. 76)

bears a close comparison with Magwitch's:

> I am not a going fur to tell you my life, like a song or a story-book. But to give it you short and handy, I'll put it at once into a mouthful of English. In jail and out of jail, in jail and out of jail. There you've got it. That's *my* life pretty much, down to such times as I got shipped off, arter Pip stood my friend.
>
> I've been done everything to, pretty well – except hanged. I've been

locked up, as much as a silver tea-kettle. I've been carted here and carted there, and put out of this town and put out of that town, and stuck in the stocks, and whipped and worried and drove. I've no more notion where I was born, than you have – if so much. I first become aware of myself, down in Essex, a thieving turnips for my living. Summun had run away from me – a man – a tinker – and he'd took the fire with him, and left me wery cold. (Ch. 42, p. 360)

The similarities between Joe's tale and Magwitch's help to indicate how they offer two alternative models for the development of Pip's own story. And both Joe and Magwitch, having suffered through their own fathers, act as foster parents to the orphaned child. Which will exercise the determining influence on him? Pip rejects each one in turn, but then comes to accept and love both. The complexities of their relationships, and the subtleties of these narrative echoes and distinctions, come eventually to illuminate the contradictory and painful tendencies within Pip's own character, which his fortunes both shape and reflect.

3

Scene/Subtext

Embedded narratives, such as the interpolated stories of Joe and Magwitch, are not the only structures which challenge and extend the single focus of the novel. Analogous and contrasting characters and situations are presented dramatically in scenes. These vivid episodes may seem virtually independent of their narrative context and yet carry extensive implications and repercussions beyond the moment. Just as story competes with secrecy in the novel, and the structure pits exposition against suspense, so dramatic scenes, focusing narrative and structural organisation in visible history nevertheless draw power from our paradoxical sense of what is not laid open in them, but kept hidden, as a subtext. This significance grows when separate scenes create a series. So Pip's fight with the 'pale young gentleman' (Chapter 11) links back to Magwitch's struggle with the 'young man' on the marshes (Chapter 5) and forward to the fight at the forge between Joe and Orlick (Chapter 15), then further to the terrible conflict between Pip and Orlick in the lime kiln (Chapter 53). Dickens offers some clues that this kind of cross-reference is appropriate. Orlick, we are told, 'as if he had been of no more account than the pale young gentleman, was very soon among the coal-dust' (Ch. 15, p. 142). Then, much later when Orlick attacks Pip (Chapter 53), he voices his resentment at having been 'bullied and beat', recalling old times so vividly that Pip finds 'what he did say presented pictures to me, and not mere words' (Ch. 53, p. 438). There are common passions and related motives running through these various scenes, linking resentment in social terms with sexual jealousy. Each battle is surprisingly, suddenly, fierce, beyond apparent cause: a quality which both individualises and also, paradoxically, connects, every disturbing explosion. Separately and together they reveal a depth of aggression that is dangerously ambivalent, for it risks self-destruction. Not Pip's fighting alone, but every one of these episodes exposes something that can scarcely be acknowledged at a conscious level: the capacity of the inner self for consuming violence.

A reading of the fight scenes supports both the duality of immediacy and the hidden, and the sense that they are at once 'about Pip' and not about him: that the qualities both stated and suppressed exist in Pip in just the measure that they exist in common humanity. We cannot analyse these episodes fully without being led on to discuss the use of symbol and setting and the further complexities of characterisation in the novel: individual scenes involve every aspect of the whole. Yet we can notice certain effects – as we do in reading – that demand attention and also contribute to the fascination of mystery in the work.

One striking and curious feature is the deliberate, constructed quality of the violence. Another is the oblique involvement of a non-combatant who acts as a provocative force: Miss Havisham, Estella, Mrs Joe. It is the antagonism between *Mrs Joe* and Orlick that causes the fight between her husband and his man at the forge – an enmity which turns to fascinated dependency in a way that seems psychologically plausible, rather than logically explicable, after Mrs Joe herself is attacked in a development that happens 'off-stage'. When Orlick's hostility is turned on Pip, Mrs Joe is invoked again, and Orlick holds Pip responsible for his murderous assault. Though Pip denies it, the accusation actually lodges with his own self-blame. So in both these struggles with Orlick there is an intricate correspondence between attraction and rage in the explosion of fury: a paradox that reaches beyond explanation, and yet answers to recognition. Strangely, it is this impenetrable complicity that we can watch under the process of construction in the dramatic build-up of Mrs Joe's hysteria. Her preposterous rage is both comically demonstrative and at the same time a signal of unspoken psychological processes.

Pip's sister has already been established as a harpy, ready with her hand, her stick, or the tar-bottle to distribute a taste of medicine. She is a figure of fury from the first. Her intervention between Joe and Orlick on the question of a half-holiday for the worker seems nevertheless oddly gratuitous. Pip shows her like a demonic voyeur, 'silent', 'a most unscrupulous spy and listener' (Ch. 15, p. 141), looking in (not out) at one of the windows. She is an intruder. Orlick infuriates her by recognising the perverse nature of her interference: ' "You'd be everybody's master, if you durst," retorted Orlick, with an ill-favoured grin' (*ibid.*). There is a sexual taunt here, and Mrs Joe does nothing to deflect it by 'beginning to work herself into a mightly rage' (*ibid.*). Her exclamations mount through repetition to a kind of verbal weapon – although the chief grammatical form is interrogative, they do not invite any exchange of ideas. Meanwhile, against her hysteria, Pip's narrative maintains an orderly, cool discretion, asking for an analytical, and not an emotional, response:

> Each of these exclamations was a shriek; and I must remark of my sister, what is equally true of all the violent women I have ever seen, that passion was no excuse for her, because it is undeniable that instead of lapsing into passion, she consciously and deliberately took extraordinary pains to force herself into it, and became blindly furious by regular stages. . . . (Ch. 15, p. 142)

Since narratives are made of words, Mrs Joe's screams are the most direct representation of her passion, and Dickens gives us a good two paragraphs of them. But he also throws in some appropriate gestures: 'Here my sister, after a fit of clappings and screamings, beat her hands upon her bosom and upon her knees, and threw her cap off, and pulled her hair down – which were the last stages on her road to frenzy.' Having provoked battle, she 'dropped insensible at the window (but . . . had seen the fight first, I think)' (Ch. 15, p. 143). Nothing remains but for her to be carried into the house, her hands clenched in Joe's hair, before 'that singular calm and silence which succeeds all uproars'. This hush marks the end of the scene, as the silent spy signalled its beginning. It is Mrs Joe's passion that has been exorcised, although not by her – an emotion compounded by social and sexual strains – and it is a similar emotion that will break out again later in Orlick, when he becomes the focus of frustrated ambition. There is no question that these are *their* feelings, and a complex relationship between them rests on this; yet it is also true that Pip too is subject to just such frustration, though never quite such rage.

The hallucinatory eruption of the fights brings Pip's memory to life with the vividness of dreams. This excitement both stretches and elides the distance of first-person narrative: stressing the 'otherness' of the personal history, and yet making it accessible to us in the shared territory of nightmare. Another 'scenic' technique attacks the problem of textual distance comically, using exaggeration to heighten the sense of artifice. Here the narrator stands with us ironically viewing his younger self. A fine example comes in Chapter 30 and the encounter with Trabb's boy. As Pip, visiting the old town, walks the length of the high street, his old adversary performs an extended improvisation on the theme of the snob's progress. Form and content collude in this piece of street theatre to point a damaging analogy between the two young men which is all the funnier as both parties maintain the pretence of unconsciousness: the satire is supposedly unintentional on one side and unnoticed on the other.

Pip is practising this superior indifference when 'that unlimited miscreant, Trabb's boy' (Ch. 30, p. 266) crosses his path. The narrative endorses his gentlemanly air through the rhythms of his long sentence, inflated vocabulary, even internal rhymes, suggesting attempted dignity. Into this pomposity – into the very sentence rhythms – breaks the panting activity of the boy. Instead of periodic construction through subordinate clauses, there comes a sequence of concatenated main clauses. Finally, direct speech interrupts the narrative with rhetorical mockery:

> Deeming that a serene and unconscious contemplation of him would best beseem me, and would be mostly likely to quell his evil mind, I advanced with that expression of countenance, and was rather congratulating myself on my success, when suddenly the knees of Trabb's boy smote together, his hair uprose, his cap fell off, he trembled violently in every limb, staggered out into the road, and, crying to the populace, 'Hold me! I'm so frightened!' feigned to be in a paroxysm of terror and contrition, occasioned by the dignity of my appearance. (Ch. 30, p. 266)

This satirical attack culminates in Trabb's boy prostrating

himself in the dust as a humiliatingly literal response to Pip's pride. No sooner has our hero passed on than his tormentor reappears – again feigning a chance encounter, with devastating effects: 'With a shock he became aware of me, and was severely visited as before; but this time his motion was rotatory, and he staggered round and round me with knees more afflicted, and with uplifted hands as if beseeching for mercy' (*ibid.*).

In the third engagement Trabb's boy varies his satirical strategy: instead of a ballet of obsequious cringing he mimics the strutting gentleman. The lively detail of the narrative, purporting to record Pip's response, actually recreates Trabb's boy's attack in all its inventive accuracy:

> Words cannot state the amount of aggravation and injury wreaked upon me by Trabb's boy, when, passing abreast of me, he pulled up his shirt collar, twined his side-hair, stuck an arm akimbo, and smirked extravagantly by, wriggling his elbow and body, and drawling to his attendants, 'Don't know yah, don't know yah, pon my soul don't know yah!' (Ch. 30, p. 267)

The comic artifice of performance here ironically points up the theme of self-recognition: blatancy and subtlety are fused together in inescapable torment.

4

Symbols/Signals

Symbols, images and motifs, like dramatic scenes, crop up suddenly in the novel, but often carry the resonance of recurrent or connecting use. Several critics have selected individual motifs and traced these patterns, concluding that in each case Dickens is doing something which cannot be called either symbolist or naturalist: he brings out the mystery in familiar things, and signals how near and how recognisable too is the strange and potent. So Barbara Hardy shows that 'Food is used to define various aspects of love, pride, social ambition, and gratitude, and the meals are often carefully placed in order to underline and explain motivation and development' (*The Moral Art of Dickens*, p. 140). Harry Stone points out

> an elaborate network of hand imagery that links half the characters of
> *Great Expectations* in a secret freemasonry of hands. One is constantly
> astonished by the magical ceremony of hands, for though plain to view, it
> is virtually invisible: it merges with one might almost say it loses itself
> in – the book's compelling realism. (*Dickens and the Invisible World:*
> *Fairy Tales, Fantasy, and Novel-Making*, p. 333)

Dorothy Van Ghent extends the scope of imagery through 'the animation of inanimate objects' ('The Dickens world: A view from Todgers's', p. 420). Just as the boundaries between the human and the objective world are challenged by this technique, so vision and dream merge different levels of reality in what is 'seen'. Flames, lamps, looking-glasses, offer vital glimpses which may be phenomenal or imagined – and may be equally 'true'. The conditions of experience are influential: place and weather carry meaning. Even everyday objects – an iron file, dustpan and brush, shark-head screws, the village finger-post – may be signals – accurate, or misleading. Notes, books, even knitting fingers, transmit messages in a variety of languages. The text is punctuated with questions, and with lies and fictions: deliberate half-truths, riddles, and secrets. Pip (who is a persistent reader) is both a blunderer and a 'visionary boy – or man' (Ch. 44, p. 377).

It is this double quality in Pip that the novel opens out. And Pip, as man and boy, narrator and protagonist, stumbler and seer, does the same for the novel form. Mediating between the author and the text (as narrator) and between the narrative and the reader, he is both the fictive controller and victim of its secrets. In neither of these functions, however, is Pip, or are we, immune from the mysteries of the novel: mysteries which are rather deepened than abolished as secrecy is overcome. The signals of the text may be interpreted, the languages translated, names recognised, questions answered, lies and fictions set aside, but the 'wonderful inconsistency' (Ch. 17, p. 156) remains, defying analysis.

Dickens's symbolism focuses the question of critical approaches to the novel because it seems both 'natural' and artful. How we appraise it depends therefore on our fundamental sense of how the novel works, how far the author controls the process and what is the part of the reader in the production or reception of the text. Truth, meaning, communication, perception are raised as technical issues which cannot be taken for granted. They are also, of course, central themes in *Great Expectations*. Yet another aspect of the work is the resistance to analysis expressed in fairy-tale, magic and dream. Reading the symbolism of the novel involves both active interpretation and submission to its charm. These two processes establish the distinction and the vital interconnection between the outer and the inner world, society and dream.

Appraising this duality allows for every degree of critical sophistication from simple imaginative enthusiasm to dispassionate theories of socio-political or psychiatric analysis. The novel works by integrating such different (and not necessarily advancing) levels of understanding. In symbolism – as also in characterisation – Dickens moves easily between the obvious and recognisable, and the strange, complex and mysterious.

The opening of the novel encourages a symbolist apprehension, through the juxtaposition of birth and death, beginning in a graveyard. The imaginative power of the elements, light and darkness, is enhanced through cold and hunger. The primitive motif of fire signals home. Gradually, social and moral issues will be objectified in locations such as the forge, Satis House, Jaggers's chambers, or Walworth. Magwitch's irons and Miss Havisham's wedding dress act as symbols of their status and their natures. From such observations to extended analysis of recurrent motifs is an easy development: the novel asks us, for example, to connect the 'two fat sweltering one pound notes' (Ch. 10, p. 107) passed on to Pip with the 'clean and new' notes (Ch. 39, p. 336) he returns. We may then think of the two guineas he offers Trabb's boy for rescuing him from the kilns (Ch. 53, p. 443), and recall the £25 premium Miss Havisham pays for his apprenticeship, and the undisclosed sum Pip makes available to fund Herbert's partnership with Clarriker – not to mention the £500 per annum which Pip learns (Ch. 36, p. 307) he is to live on until the donor of his fortune appears. Added together, these transactions amount to an economic system, but in that light they remain no more than a symbol: the values they express are not essentially financial but moral, and have to do with the exercise of the power and the reticence of true charity.

The disguises of significance range from plain ordinariness to comic incongruity, and from realism to the supernatural. Things and names, ghosts and dreams, questions and lies, distinctive idioms and a series of paradoxes co-exist in this range of expressive and suggestive techniques: some obvious, some positively obstructive. In tracing them it is helpful to bear in mind some of the textual clues littering *Great Expectations* which prompt curiosity and interpretation. First comes the ambiguous title itself, but this signal pun is extended through paradoxes of which Pip is half, or sometimes wholly, aware: 'that wonderful inconsistency' of love (Ch. 17, p. 156); a 'keen sense of incongruity' (Ch. 27, p. 240) in his relations with Joe; Estella speaking of herself as if she were someone else (Ch. 33, p. 286), and laughing in such a way that Pip 'could not doubt its being genuine, and yet it seemed too much for the occasion. I thought there must really be something more here than I knew; she saw the thought in my mind, and answered it' (Ch. 33, p. 287). Amongst Pip's friends a 'gay fiction' of enjoyment is opposed to a 'skeleton truth' (Ch. 34, p. 294). On the other hand, Dickens happily presents a moment of innocent gaiety when Pip tries to find out what Wemmick's father thinks of Jaggers, and is confounded by the Aged P's response: 'I roared that name at him. He threw me into the greatest confusion by laughing heartily and replying in a very sprightly manner, "No, to be sure; you're right" ' (Ch. 37, p. 312) – a retort wonderfully bringing affirmation out of a negative. Later, Pip's haughty dismissal of Magwitch using the politely coercive formula 'but surely you must understand' (Ch. 39, p. 334) rounds on him when Magwitch picks up and repeats his words, with more than polite significance. What Pip 'must understand' is at this stage too much for him to express: 'Words cannot tell what a sense I had, at the same time, of the dreadful mystery that he was to me' (Ch. 40, p. 353). The urge to 'understand' and the apprehension of 'dreadful mystery' constitute the two strains of the novel. They underlie such potent warnings as Wemmick's 'Don't break cover' (Ch. 45, p. 384), and the irresistible summons from Orlick that tempts Pip to do just that:

> For, I really had not been myself since the receipt of the letter; it had so bewildered me ensuing on the hurry of the morning. The morning hurry and flutter had been great, for, long and anxiously as I had waited for Wemmick, his hint had come like a surprise at last. And now, I began to wonder at myself for being in the coach, and to doubt whether I had sufficient reason for being there, and to consider whether I should get out presently and go back, and to argue against ever heeding an anonymous communication, and, in short, to pass through all those phases of contradiction and indecision to which I suppose very few hurried people are strangers. (Ch. 52, pp. 430–1).

It is Magwitch, on the point of freedom, the point of recapture and imprisonment, who calmly expresses the possibility of 'Negative Capability' in the face of mystery. His language is both simply naturalistic and deeply symbolic:

> I was a thinking through my smoke just then, that we can no more see to the bottom of the next few hours, than we can see to the bottom of this river what I catches hold of. Nor yet we can't no more hold their tide

than I can hold this. And it's run through my fingers and gone, you see! (Ch. 54, p. 448)

Great Expectations moves towards this wise inexpectancy through a series of prompts and warnings over meaning. The world of the novel is charged with significance (as Magwitch shows, using his pipe and the River Thames). Country and city, land and sea, earth and air seem to polarise the possibilities of experience in terms of innocence or sophistication and guilt, humility or ambition, which are further located in specific places. The forge stands for a set of values (also embodied in Joe) based on honest work; it is contrasted with Satis House, whose dominant character-istic (seen also in Miss Havisham) is closure. Putting it this simply, we can see how far from direct opposition this relationship is. There is no straightforward choice. Rather, oblique comparisons allow for the eventual possibility of Pip's coming 'home' to both places at the end of the novel, not to stay in either, but to embrace the values of love in both its homely and visionary aspects. And Jaggers's place of business (pointedly named Little Britain) offers an alternative model from the forge. The office is set about with death masks, the icons of legacy, which could be seen as symboli-cally comparable with Magwitch's ambitions for Pip: to make him 'his gentleman', a kind of *alter ego* to the transported convict. Jaggers also has a closet, where he 'washed his clients off' (Ch. 26, p. 233) like Pontius Pilate. Another place evidently imbued with symbolic value is the lime kiln (Chapter 53) with its destructive fires, darkness and solitude. On the other hand, we have Wal-worth, the Pockets' household, Pip's bachelor rooms, and Clara's lodgings, each showing what a home may be, depending on the values governing the household. Such examples have both narrative and symbolic value, though either may predominate. Walworth, for example, is developed to the point of comic grotesque, undermining in a far from subtle way the value of 'portable property' which Wemmick professes to espouse. This does not destroy the character of Wemmick, however, since his mask is not an exact fit for his finer features. In contrast, Pip's room at the forge exactly corresponds to his feelings of home there. We do not sense any contrivance, even when he explicity reflects on it:

> When I got into my little room, I sat down and took a long look at it, as a mean little room that I should soon be parted from and raised above, for ever. It was furnished with fresh young remembrances too, and even at the same moment I fell into much the same confused division of mind between it and the rooms to which I was going, as I had been in so often between the forge and Miss Havisham's, and Biddy and Estella. (Ch. 18, p. 172)

It is this inwardness of response, bound up with memory, even during the course of the narrative, that endows place with meaning. Most curious in this respect is Satis House, which enshrines memories for Miss Havisham, and fantasies for Pip: there is a tension between these two possibilities which accentuates the danger of both modes of apprehension. Fantastic enough in its first appearance, Miss Havisham's is immediately *re*created in transformed guise in the text through Pip's 'lies' to his sister: fictions no more extravagant than what he has witnessed. It is a place of 'dreadful mystery', most believable as it so flagrantly challenges belief.

Pip's narrative has a tendency towards extremes: an imaginative pattern of acceleration. This corresponds in the reading process to the experience of memory for the narrator: bringing the remote into actuality, not instantaneously, but by perceptible stages. The sense of movement involved is not accidental but effectual. So at the opening, time is made visible through light and darkness, naturally alternating, but in a rhythm dictated by psychological rather than terrestrial laws. A mood, as well as an hour, is suggested when Pip tells us, 'My first most vivid and broad impression of the identity of things seems to me to have been gained on a memorable raw afternoon towards evening' (Ch. 1, p. 35). The preposition 'towards' indicates the movement of the narrative, which passes within this short chapter to lurid nightfall:

> The marshes were just a long black horizontal line then, as I stopped to look after him; and the river was just another horizontal line, not nearly so broad nor yet so black; and the sky was just a row of long angry red lines and dense black lines intermixed. (Ch. 1, p. 39)

Not only the colours but the lines of this picture express rage and fear, yet the landscape itself has not changed topographically. What we perceive are feelings latent in Pip's world, which the terrifying encounter with the escaped convict has brought out. The transformation of the initial scene to this is shockingly brusque yet, with the movement of the day itself, apparently inevitable. The oscillation from evening to morning and back which begins here illuminates both the visible and the inner world of the child in strong tones.

When Pip enters Satis House 'the first thing I noticed was, that the passages were all dark, and that she had left a candle burning there' (Ch. 8, p. 86). Miss Havisham's trauma cannot obliterate time, but she can convert it to perpetual night. In this darkness both the damage of her pain and the force of her will are externalised. In Pip's apprehension, however, they are again absorbed into an inner world: the one to which the narrative alone gives us entry: 'Daylight never entered the house as to my thoughts and remembrance of it, any more than as to the actual fact' (Ch. 17, p. 152). Later, the explicit judgement of Miss Havisham's artificial night is both moral and psychological. Pip's understanding hovers between clinical analysis and homiletic exegesis (though his restraint from speaking out would seem closer to psychiatric than religious practice):

> I knew not how to answer, or how to comfort her. . . .But that, in shutting out the light of day, she had shut out infinitely more; that, in seclusion, she had secluded herself from a thousand natural and healing influences; that, her mind, brooding solitary, had grown diseased, as all minds do and must and will that reverse the appointed order of their maker; I knew equally well. (Ch. 49, p. 411)

The force of darkness and light for Pip is more varied. From the first afternoon and the next misty morning, he is frequently caught between the extremes, in partial obscurity, and this is as much psychological as moral – besides its literal meaning. Miss Havisham's darkness is penetrated by a candle, which ironically foreshadows the consuming flames that will destroy her living tomb. Pip's dimness, however, is subject to sudden flares of illumination. When he escorts Estella to Richmond, his conversation about Jaggers is abruptly interrupted by one such moment of brilliance, and the effect is very strange:

> I should have been chary of discussing my guardian too freely even with
> her; but I should have gone on with the subject so far as to describe the
> dinner in Gerrard-street, if we had not then come into a sudden glare of
> gas. It seemed, while it lasted, to be all alight and alive with that
> inexplicable feeling I had had before; and when we were out of it, I was
> as much dazed for a few moments as if I had been in Lightning. (Ch. 33,
> p. 289)

Only on a second reading can we grasp the hidden explanation of
this sensation: that Estella is the daughter of the servant Pip first
met at that dinner in Gerrard Street. At first, this episode seems
inexplicably portentous. The 'glare' of danger, associated with too
much light, might seem supernatural – except for its easy association of literal distortion with perceptual dazzlement: an imaginative *frisson* which is both symbolist and naturalistic too. What
we experience is the immanence of meaning here, and not the
interpretation: the moment 'all alight and alive'.

Lamplight illuminates Pip's encounters with Magwitch in
London, with an optical precision we should now think of as
cinematic, though for Dickens the most we could claim is that it
was theatrical or painterly, involving dramatic heightening through
point of view and chiaroscuro. In Chapter 39 (p. 322) we are told
that the staircase lights are all blown out by the storm, and when
Pip hears someone climbing out of the darkness, he stands with his
reading lamp at the top of the stairs, while the stranger comes into
its circle, then out of it. The glimpse is brilliantly precise. Exactly
realistic, unarguably symbolic. Not one to waste such a superb
effect, Dickens recalls and reverses it in Chapter 46 when
Magwitch stands 'holding a light over the stair-rail to light us
down stairs' (p. 392). The point of the echo is precisely in Pip's
recognition of it: this is how he learns to read his experience.

Another dramatic moment of recognition–as–insight comes out
of deep darkness in Chapter 53. Again it is the visual precision that
first strikes us. The very rhythm of the sentences conveys the
movement of the eyes (the only movement possible, since Pip is
bound and gagged). Urgency is extended by this device. Illumination is fitful, partial, gradual; then bewildering; finally it is

complete, mutual, potent – Pip recognises his old antagonist, looking at him:

> The sudden exclusion of the night and the substitution of black darkness in its place, warned me that the man had closed a shutter. After groping about for a little, he found the flint and steel he wanted, and began to strike a light. I strained my sight upon the sparks that fell among the tinder, and upon which he breathed and breathed, match in hand, but I could only see his lips, and the blue point of the match; even those, but fitfully. The tinder was damp – no wonder there – and one after another the sparks died out.
>
> The man was in no hurry, and struck again with the flint and steel. As the sparks fell thick and bright about him, I could see his hands, and touches of his face, and could make out that he was seated and bending over the table; but nothing more. Presently I saw his blue lips again, breathing on the tinder, and then a flare of light flashed up, and showed me Orlick.
>
> Whom I had looked for, I don't know. I had not looked for him. Seeing him, I felt that I was in a dangerous strait indeed, and I kept my eyes upon him.
>
> He lighted the candle from the flaring match with great deliberation, and dropped the match, and trod it out. Then, he put the candle away from him on the table so that he could see me, and sat with his arms folded on the table and looked at me. (Ch. 53, pp. 434–5)

The control of the field of vision throughout this passage is measured and exact. The first effect is dramatic, but the reverberations of the prose add to its deeper effects. 'Groping about', straining, seeing, looking, making out, refer to a process of enquiry more far-reaching than superficial recognition. It is important to stress that this climactic encounter between the antagonists allows both to face what has lain hidden through a large stretch of the novel, and will indeed remain, however weakened, even after this. The forces embodied in Orlick cannot wholly be exorcised from Pip himself.

Place and light work both naturally and as symbols in the novel. Pip feels this and we do too. The transition between these levels of apprehension demonstrates Pip's sensitivity and insight. For the reader it has an ambivalent effect: at once encouraging imaginative excitement and intimacy with the text, and also obstructing this identification by stimulating our critical awareness, asking us to 'read' signs. Other motifs too work in this dual way. Objects, images, forms of words and the merest intimations of half-perceived truths – things which are superficially very different – can be grouped together as symbolic systems. They are included in the language of the whole novel, but they each have their own idioms, their own tone, and different degrees of obviousness or abstruseness: hand symbolism, ironmongery, legal jargon, names, fictions, lies, dreams, for example; they are all themselves, but also signals of something else. They make up the recognisable world of the novel, but they also point to its fictive quality. They bring Pip's history to life, and they obstruct our simple wish to believe it. Instead they ask us to read, to interpret, to understand.

The first hands in *Great Expectations* illustrate this. We see them on the opening page – and yet they do not exist. They are metaphorical hands: an image created by Pip's fancy, taken out of a common figure of speech, but given new vividness by the context in which he relocates them. These hands become preposterous, comic, even grotesque, if the metaphor is literalised. They are the hands Pip imagines for his infant brothers, whom he knows only through their memorial stones. In his childish fantasy the grave pockets up these unsuccessful entrepreneurs like men of the world swallowed up in a premature takeover:

> To five little stone lozenges, each about a foot and a half long, which were arranged in a neat row beside their grave, and were sacred to the memory of five little brothers of mine – who gave up trying to get a living, exceedingly early in that universal struggle – I am indebted for a belief I religiously entertained that they had all been born on their backs with their hands in their trousers-pockets, and had never taken them out in this state of existence. (Ch. 1, p. 35)

These gentlemanly (but lifeless) hands are briskly succeeded, at the opening of the second chapter, by the 'hard and heavy' (p. 39) hand of Mrs Joe Gargery. Brought up 'by hand', Pip again interprets the verbal formula in accordance with his direct experience, 'Having at that time to find out for myself what the expression meant' (Ch. 2, p. 39). Literal and metaphorical are comically locked together.

The technique is similar, but the effect is different, when Pip runs to the door of the forge (Ch. 4, p. 61) only to bump into a party of soliders holding out a pair of handcuffs. The phenomenal world seems magically attuned to his subconscious. Real handcuffs for his secret guilt. It is a terrifying apparition, yet there is also something comic in this prompt and literal turn of events. Pip's qualms are acute but (to our eyes) unnecessary, and his reading of this encounter is equally mistaken: the cuffs are not for him.

Dickens makes ironic capital out of the disparity between literal and symbolic. But the immanence of meaning in the concrete world persists. When Estella calls his hands coarse (Ch. 8, p. 90), Pip feels branded. Jaggers's scented hand physically signals a moral consciousness of defilement (Ch. 11, p. 112). Miss Havisham (*ibid.*) has a 'withered hand', Biddy (Ch. 17, p. 156) a 'comfortable hand, though roughened by work'; Joe, when asked to let Pip go, 'laid his hand upon my shoulder with the touch of a woman' (Ch. 18, p. 168). Gestures speak. Shaking hands with Pumblechook (Ch. 19, p. 180) is a hypocritical performance, but kissing Miss Havisham's hand 'came naturally' (Ch. 19, p. 184). Meeting Wemmick, Pip 'put out my hand, and Mr Wemmick at first looked at it as if he thought I wanted something. Then he looked at me, and said, correcting himself, "To be sure! Yes. You're in the habit of shaking hands?" ' (Ch. 21, p. 197). The question not only reveals something about Wemmick and his London world (which is what it does for Pip at the time) but serves as a prompt to us in reading this language of gesture: a hint that nothing can be taken for granted.

Hand signals so habitual that they are virtually naturalistic provide a ground for the special significance of hands in the plot of *Great Expectations*. It is through the resemblance of their hands that Pip links Molly with Estella. They are not superficially alike: Estella has the white hands of a lady, Molly the sinewy grip of a man, and wrists disfigured and scarred. What connects them – through a kind of gestural pun – is an action common to both: the movement of knitting fingers. Seeing Estella do this, Pip interprets the gesture as a message encoded in another language; but it gives away more than she knows, or Pip is yet ready to guess:

> Estella, pausing a moment in her knitting with her eyes upon me, and then going on, I fancied that I read in the action of her fingers, as plainly

as if she had told me in the dumb alphabet, that she perceived I had discovered my real benefactor. (Ch. 44, p. 372)

The curious thing is that the same signal has two meanings, though Estella herself is only half aware of one. When Pip sees Molly's fingers knit together, he recognises that she is Estella's *mother* (Ch. 48, p. 403); but the original gesture was of course connected with Pip's benefactor – the man eventually revealed as Estella's father.

The language of hands is most poignantly developed for Pip with Magwitch at the end (Ch. 56, pp. 469–70). Gentle pressure, a clasp, two hands covering another, the hand on the breast or at the lips speak when words have failed the dying man. This is prayer: the communication of love, through hands joined together. Within three pages, it is Pip on his sickbed and Joe beside him who use the same means of expression (Ch. 57, p. 473). And finally, Pip and Estella take hands, leaving the garden of Satis House like Milton's couple leaving Eden: 'I took her hand in mine, and we went out of the ruined place' (Ch. 59, p. 493).

The possibilities of expression and significance in hands are subtle and various. Not so, we might think, with the concrete world of solid objects. Yet Dickens attaches significance to simple things with a kind of imaginative muscularity which asserts the interest of relating the inner to the outer world. When Miss Havisham tells Pip he should now be apprenticed to Joe, Mrs Joe runs amok in the forge. The obliquity, as well as the fury, of her response tells us that her frustrated ambition is personal. It is because she feels that her life has been sacrificed to Pip's welfare that she harbours this anger: hence its expression through the tools of domesticity, turned into weapons of the subtext. There is a witty counterpoint in the text between the discreet use of indirect speech – a kind of stylistic decorum – and the open outrage of Mrs Joe's direct action:

She asked me and Joe whether we supposed she was door-mats under our feet, and how we dared to use her so, and what company we graciously thought she *was* fit for? When she had exhausted a torrent of such inquiries, she threw a candlestick at Joe, burst into a loud sobbing, got out the dustpan – which was always a very bad sign – put on her coarse apron, and began cleaning up to a terrible extent. (Ch. 12, p. 126)

Even a candlestick or dustpan and brush may act as a 'very bad sign' to the alert intelligence. And such things may also be misread. After his first year of apprenticeship Pip proposes to show Miss Havisham that he remembers her, and Joe enthusiastically entertains the possibilities of a small keepsake: a set of horsehoes, for example,

> 'Or even,' said he, 'if you was helped to knocking her up a new chain for the front door – or say a gross or two of shark-headed screws for general use – or some light fancy article, such as a toasting-fork when she took her muffins – or a gridiron when she took a sprat or such like –'. (Ch. 15, p. 139)

Joe's professionalism gives him a new fluency, but he is not slow to reverse this production of examples, advising against such exposure:

> 'Well,' said Joe . . . 'if I was yourself, Pip, I wouldn't. No, I would *not*. For what's a door-chain when she's got one always up? And shark-headers is open to misrepresentations. And if it was a toasting-fork you'd go into brass and do yourself no credit. And the oncommonest workman can't show himself oncommon in a gridiron – for a gridiron IS a gridiron,' said Joe, steadfastly impressing it upon me, as if he were endeavouring to rouse me from a fixed delusion, 'and you may haim at what you like, but a gridiron it will come out, either by your leave or against your leave, and you can't help yourself –'. (*ibid.*)

Amidst the ironmongery of the novel, the most potent and recurrent items are the convict's irons and the file he uses to free himself. Their terrible significance is suggested by their unpredictable reappearance in quite different contexts. Through the first five chapters the fetters and file are associated with Magwitch and with the guilt Pip feels in helping him. Ironically, to free Magwitch is to forge a bond with him from which he cannot go free. Then in Chapter 10, without warning, Pip sees a stranger at the public bar gesturing to him:

> It was not a verbal remark, but a proceeding in dumb show, and was pointedly addressed to me. He stirred his rum-and-water pointedly at me, and he tasted his rum-and-water pointedly at me. And he stirred it and he tasted it: not with a spoon that was brought to him, but *with a file*. (Ch. 10, p. 106)

The same dread stranger crops up again in Chapter 28, wearing irons – 'irons of a pattern I knew well' (p. 248) and speaking to his companion of the episode in the pub. He is not there for the plot, nor even (primarily) to assist the memory of a reader of the novel-in-parts, but as the uncanny apparition of Pip's accusing conscience, stirring unquietly even when his fortunes seem secure. It is because of this guilt that Pip is curiously unsurprised when he finds the weapon used to fell his sister was none other than the very leg-iron he had freed his convict from. His response is thoughtful:

> Knowing what I knew, I set up an inference of my own here. I believed the iron to be my convict's iron – the iron I had seen and heard him filing at, on the marshes – but my mind did not accuse him of having put it to its latest use. For, I believed one of two other persons to have become possessed of it, and to have turned it to this cruel account. Either Orlick, or the strange man who had shown me the file. (Ch. 16, p. 148)

This inference will eventually be justified by Orlick's confession at the lime kiln (Chapter 53). But another evil presence will also be associated with the file motif, when Magwitch tells his own story, and describes the hateful Compeyson as a swindler, forger, fence, and traitor: ' "He'd no more heart than a iron file, he was as cold as death, and he had the head of the Devil afore mentioned" ' (Ch. 42, p. 362).

The contamination and persistence of guilt in Pip's world is hinted by the recurrence of irons and file: crude but effective signals. There are other devices too which work not despite but through their obviousness. The finger-post at the edge of Pip's home town (a variant on the hand motif, perhaps?) 'points out' the moral values of the forge. Pip lays his hand on it and speaks to it as a 'dear, dear friend!' (Ch. 19, p. 186) even though he has just left Joe rather casually. This moment 'smote upon my heart again' (Ch. 30, p. 271) later, when Herbert is asking him to think carefully about his feelings for Estella. In the first appearance, the post has a naturalistic appropriateness – Pip is walking past it – but in a different context that aspect has fallen away, leaving only its hidden meaning, accessible to us through Pip's own apprehension of it.

Names are signs, and not simply labels, in *Great Expectations*:

the information they give may be only indirectly revealing: requiring to be decoded, interpreted, read. Pip introduces himself rather formally, almost genealogically, through a name which both is and is not that of his father. His 'infant tongue' has transformed it ('infant' means, etymologically, non-speaking) into his own: the name which distinguishes his personal identity, and which he is to keep through all his changes of fortunes – keep, indeed, as a condition of his expectations. There is a gentle parody of this constancy when we see Joe 'reading' – the only letters he can find in any text are his own version of his name: ' "Why, here's a J," said Joe, "and a O equal to anythink! Here's a J and a O, Pip, and a J–O, Joe!" ' (Ch. 7, p. 75). In contrast with this simple integrity, an alias may indicate perversity. The first accusation against Orlick rests on this:

> Now, Joe kept a journeyman at weekly wages whose name was Orlick. He pretended that his christian name was Dolge – a clear impossibility – but he was a fellow of that obstinate disposition that I believe him to have been the prey of no delusion in this particular, but wilfully to have imposed that name upon the village as an affront to its understanding. (Ch. 15, pp. 139–40)

This indignant observation from Pip (whose own name, we recall, is self-made) follows immediately on an incident in which he himself alters a 'christian name': if Joe were to give him a half-holiday, he says, ' "I think I would go up-town and make a call on Miss Est – Havisham." "Which her name," said Joe gravely, "ain't Estavisham, Pip, unless she have been rechristened" ' (Ch. 15, p. 139). The slip voices the subtext, betraying Pip's secret desire. Elsewhere, misnaming seems shameful; Estella taunts Pip for a solecism: ' "He calls the knaves, Jacks, this boy!" ' (Ch. 8, p. 90). But Magwitch's name is a secret beyond the *faux pas*. For much of the novel it is unknown, and Pip's mistake derives from this. Then, when he finally learns the identity of his benefactor, the convict is using a false name: Provis. He is also known by the description 'Of New South Wales': but only when he is in fact in London, in hiding. This subterfuge surrounding Magwitch's name increases the excitement of the suspense story, but it also expresses symbolically the emotions of guilt, fear, pain and loss associated with him in

Pip's experience. For himself, Abel Magwitch's name is the first thing he knows (the Christian name helps us think of him as more sinned against than sinning, for Abel was the first victim, in the fallen world). And for Pip too, eventually, identifying Magwitch is a triumph, for it tells him something vital about Estella: something dangerous to reveal, but necessary to know.

The search for knowledge and the disguises of truth are complicated by the variety of signs and symbols in the novel, yet there is a constant movement towards understanding. Questions are a feature of the text. The convict interrogates Pip in the graveyard at the opening, and Pip in turn asks at home about the firing, the Hulks and prisoners; Mrs Joe answers him with the logic of the text, rather than jurisprudence: ' "People are put in the Hulks because they murder, and because they rob, and forge, and do all sorts of bad; and they always begin by asking questions" ' (Ch. 2, p. 46). It is true that questioning is bound up with guilt in this work, because its secrets are guilty. Nevertheless, self-knowledge is necessary to development. Biddy's quiet questions clarify Pip's feelings for Estella (Chapter 17), yet while his understanding grows it does not diminish or alter his love, for 'how could I, a poor dazed village lad, avoid that wonderful inconsistency into which the best and wisest of men fall every day?' (Ch. 17, p. 156). This 'wonderful inconsistency' inspires Pip's researches into Estella's origins, and yet provokes no adverse reaction when he learns what they are. Pip's drive to know is quite different from the suspicious legal catechisms of Jaggers, which are designed as much to conceal as to reveal the truth.

Just as questions bear a strange power in a text heavily dependent on secrecy, so lies and fictions are mysteriously revealing. Pip's encounter with Satis House (Chapter 8) is so challenging that he defends himself, both there and afterwards, by reconstructing his history through lies. But Pip's lies are no stranger than the fictions of the text. Instead of assailing or correcting it, they contribute to it. Pip as a story-teller is part of Pip's history. A remarkable part, because he displays particular self-consciousness in this, and it produces a piquant counterpoint of honesty and invention: two aspects of imaginative awareness which turn out not to be opposed, but capable of coexisting. So the fencing between Pip and Miss Havisham when they first meet is both aggressive and co-operative, as their relations will be till the end: ' "Look at me," said Miss Havisham. "You are not afraid of a woman who has never seen the sun since you were born?" I regret to state that I was not afraid of telling the enormous lie comprehended in the answer "No" ' (Ch. 8, p. 88). When he gets home, it is Pumblechook and Mrs Joe who are asking the questions, and Pip's lies grow in proportion to their aggressive curiosity. Yet his version of the day, embellished with black coach and bright flags, swords and dogs and candles, scarcely displaces the extravagance we have just read; rather, it acts as a kind of decorative coda. It is only with Joe that Pip feels any compunction, and they arrive soon at an understanding beyond 'metaphysics', 'namely, that lies is lies. Howsoever they come, they didn't ought to come, and they come from the father of lies, and work round to the same' (Ch. 9, p. 100). Nevertheless, the novel takes delight in its inventions (as the round repetitiveness and balance of Joe's denunciation demonstrates well), and even Joe sees the advantage of elaborating the truth on occasion. When he comes back from Satis House (Ch. 13, pp. 130–1), he brings Mrs Joe a complimentary greeting from Miss Havisham concocted entirely in his own head, and delivers it with cunning hesitations worthy of a master story-teller.

Joe's message works brilliantly because it answers the unspoken requirements of the situation. He has a grasp of the 'subtext' in his wife's questions. His understanding indeed enables Joe throughout the novel to behave with exemplary and self-effacing dignity. Even when he jeopardises this (at Biddy's behest) by stepping out of his sphere to visit Pip in London (Chapter 27), he knows what he is risking and why it has gone wrong and he declines firmly to compromise himself again. There is a sense in which Joe has already arrived at the point which Pip through the narrative is aiming for. His marrying Biddy just before Pip thinks of doing so demonstrates this. Yet Joe, for all his goodness and self-consistency, cannot equal Pip, 'that visionary boy – or man', because his dreams are less potent. Pip's fancies and fantasies haunt the text as visible ghosts, memories and apprehensions, and the indefinable distinctions between these phenomena indicate how closely the imagined and perceived worlds intertwine, how lies and truths are interfused in fictions.

Ghosts appear both to focus emotions and to shadow the plot of *Great Expectations*. They move between the inner and the outer world, aligning mere secrecy with the deeper mystery. Partly through their agency, the concepts of reality and unreality are loosed from the ties with substance and identified with idea, form, dream, the quick of imagined truth.

Ironically, despite the hopeful title, the ghosts of the novel betray a preoccupation with the painful emotions of fear and desire: the two inseparable aspects of Pip's 'expectations'. The first apparition (after Pip's 'fancies' of his dead parents and small brothers) is the loud and substantial Magwitch, 'a fearful man' (Ch. 1, p. 36) starting up from among the graves. The second is the unseen menace Magwitch conjures up: 'a young man hid with me, in comparison with which young man I am a Angel' (Ch. 1, p. 38). In Magwitch's terrible threat, this young man has the secret knowledge, the vengeful persistence, of the ghost, and the capacity to 'softly creep and creep his way' to a victim. It is these qualities which make him real to Pip, and it is no surprise to him when he meets the young man in person on his return to the marshes (Chapter 3). Now, however, Magwitch is horrified. His 'fancy' has taken on physical form, dramatically embodied as Compeyson, who haunts him inescapably because he represents his own resentment. And as Magwitch cannot be free of Compeyson, so Pip will be dogged by the haunting guilt of Magwitch himself. From the start we witness the mutuality of obsession. Ghosts answer the haunted mind.

There is a fine comic version of the same pattern in Pip's experience, showing (twice over) how the mind summons its own phantoms. Pip creates his own tormentor: the boy in the canary waistcoast, whose sole *raison d'être* appears to be to remind Pip of just how miserable his wealth makes him. This boy is described as a 'monster', 'this avenging phantom', who 'haunted my existence' (Ch. 27, pp. 240–1). (There is an obvious parallel to the

Frankenstein myth invoked with Magwitch (Chapter 40, p. 354)). And this hideous embodiment of irresponsible creation aptly appears when Pip is expecting Joe on a visit in London – Joe, who has been like a father to him, and whom he will snub and neglect. When Pip goes down to the country, and again avoids Joe, his punishment is meted out by another tormenting spirit of vengeance, Trabb's boy. Like the Avenger, this deconstructive critic mimics his victim, presenting his own airs and graces grotesquely enlarged to his view. He is a doppelganger, and an embarrassment; 'a boy who excited Loathing', but uncannily invulnerable to retribution, 'a boy whom no man could hurt' (Ch. 30, p. 267).

The theatrical ghosts of *Great Expectations* move from the comic to the terrible, and from the stage to the auditorium, as their critical relevance shifts from Pip to Magwitch. The story of Wopsle's difficulties with the ghost of Hamlet's father is told by Joe on his London visit (Chapter 27) and it acts as a very oblique comment on the relations between Joe and Pip. But when Pip himself is 'haunted' at the play (Chapter 47), and by none other than that very young man of the opening chapter, it is Magwitch who is being pursued. The two dramatic occasions are connected, but their tone could scarcely be more different. First to comic, then to horrific effect, Dickens uses them to illustrate, extend and comment on the imaginative stretch of 'reality' through artistic illusion.

The challenge of artifice is keenest, however, in Miss Havisham, who makes herself her own ghost, in an existence of living death, whose sharpest pleasures are the revival and reversal of her old pain, with Estella taking vengeance on her behalf, and the anticipation of her own end, held out to her heirs in ghoulish derision. Miss Havisham looks phantasmal, dressed in white, and tattered; she lives in artificial darkness; no food is seen to pass her lips; even her movement is unnatural, as she is wheeled around her rooms, or 'walked' with a stick. From her vantage point in her intermediary world she apprehends the secret and unseen, giving her grim visions the vivid force of existence in the text: making Pip, making us, see her foreshadowed as a corpse, whether lying on her bridal table (Ch. 11, p. 117) or hanging (as he imagines her) from a beam

(Ch. 8, p. 94). She also sees mysteriously into others, and this penetration is figured imagistically through her use of mirrors. Miss Havisham openly demonstrates the processes of comparison underlying structures of characterisation in the text:

> Before she spoke again, she turned her eyes from me, and looked at the dress she wore, and at the dressing table, and finally at herself in the looking-glass.
> 'So new to him,' she muttered, 'so old to me; so strange to him, so familiar to me; so melancholy to both of us! Call Estella.' (Ch. 8, p. 89)

Much as horror and terror surround Miss Havisham and Magwitch with dreadful apparitions, so desire, not in the narrow sense of lust, but the almost impersonal extreme of longing, makes Estella the focus of dreams and visions for Pip. The emotions are different, but the imaginative intensity much the same, and its haunting effects are strangely allied. This is one of the ways in which the interrelationship of these figures is conveyed in the novel. Plot, of course, is another, and the theme of adoption; but the very inwardness, the involuntary and obsessive quality of their ghostly presences suggest how intimately all three – Magwitch, Miss Havisham and Estella – are bound up with the inmost aspects of Pip's very self.

Estella, like Magwitch, appears in the text first as a voice, and the epithet for hers is 'clear'. There is nothing supernatural about this. When Miss Havisham tells Pip to call her back, however, we learn that 'she answered at last, and her light came along the dark passage like a star' (*ibid.*). The name Estella means star, and the girl herself seems here to be made of light. Throughout the novel, she carries this radiance, as here she carries a candle; her beauty is something unwilled, even despised: an instrument answering to command, or a force summoned by longing. The dislocation of distinct aspects of Estella has some relation to the disruptive effect she has on Pip from within his heart: she provokes, and she represents, unquenchable and ungovernable emotions. But this abstract notion seems a clumsy redaction of her dynamic force. Estella proud, pretty and insulting; Estella dancing inexplicably on the casks, her back turned, and her hair spread out in her two hands

(Ch. 8, p. 93); Estella bejewelled (Ch. 11, p. 113); Estella's face seen in the fire, with her pretty eyes scorning (Ch. 14, p. 136): she is a figure of equal potency in absence or presence. Pip avows, 'In a word, it was impossible for me to separate her, in the past or in the present, from the innermost life of my life' (Ch. 29, p. 257).

The mysterious resemblance of hands which links Estella in Pip's mind with Jaggers's servant Molly becomes more than a clumsy melodramatic plot device because we apprehend it through Pip's own sense of inexplicable excitement. The textual signal of this visionary energy is the strange flashes of light accompanying his perceptions. These illuminations represent mental processes; yet they seem also in some way to symbolise Estella's power, her light. Estella's origin is a secret Pip cannot share with her, and one indeed that she need never know: it is what it means to him that matters. She is closest to and most distant from his essential self. Her preternatural beauty and coldness both add to her visionary quality. Her intractable resistance is what makes her so alluring. He can dream of her; she can (unthinkably) give herself to Bentley Drummle. Even the union of Pip and Estella at the close holds in reserve the hint of a possible separation, an unseen shadow:

> I took her hand in mine, and we went out of the ruined place; and, as the morning mists had risen long ago when I first left the forge, so the evening mists were rising now, and in all the broad expanse of tranquil light they showed to me, I saw no shadow of another parting from her. (Ch. 59, p. 493)

5

Character:
Identity/Function

Ghosts, dreams and visions help to reveal personality in *Great Expectations*. Postmodern psychoanalytic critics would see these as aspects of that divide between the symbolic and the imaginary constituting the structure of relations between the individual and the world which establishes identity, a more fundamental concept than mere personality. (Steven Connor offers such a reading in *Charles Dickens*, 1985.) We can, however, reconcile these two levels of analysis in recognising that all aspects of symbolism contribute to the delineation of character in Dickens. His first readers admired this function of his art above all others, but they thought the strength of characterisation lay in externals – such as physical description and the speech idioms – and it was widely felt that Dickens never surpassed his first novel, *Pickwick Papers*, in this. In relating the inmost to this outward phenomenal world we can now begin to account for the full complexity of characterisation in *Great Expectations*. What we find is an extraordinary range of effects, from the broadest to the most subtle: psychological, physical, rhetorical, narratological and most pervasively, structural. Only in recognising this diversity can we explain something very remarkable in the novel – the integration of individuality with reciprocity: the sense that each character is unique, and yet our understanding depends on cross-reference between them. Pip is the central character, and the others people his world. Yet they also hold our interest, they 'overlap' and distract us from Pip; the ways in which this happens help formally to indicate how socially, morally, psychologically, and so on, Pip is related to his world. These narratological divergences effectively

70

save the first person narrative from the epistemological trap of solipsism, much as Pip is saved within the novel from the moral prison of selfishness by the demands of other people. So the negotiation – formal, social, moral – between the individual and the world, the balance between assertion and reception, creates the rhythms of experience, both within the text and in the reading of it, making Pip's memories real for us. This is the process of fictional autobiography, working on and working with the reader, working at and through the text.

Character is a concept as central to the novel form as story, structure, symbol. Characters, their histories, their interrelationships, their names and identifying features have already appeared repeatedly in our discussion of *Great Expectations*; inevitably so. In changing focus here to concentrate on character, we can extend our reading in two ways: both to appreciate more of the complexity and vitality of individual characters, and to work towards an exploration of Pip himself, and the use of the first person mode of narration.

The disposition of characters who both exist independently and have a bearing on the protagonist's character too is not new in *Great Expectations*. Dickens had used this technique in *David Copperfield*, that earlier first-person novel which his friend and biographer John Forster reports Dickens carefully reread when setting out to write Pip's narrative. The idea of clarifying character traits and development through a sequence of encounters highlighting individual aspects of the self is of course much older; we find it most clearly in morality plays such as *Everyman*, or in John Bunyan's *Pilgrim's Progress*. How has Dickens adapted this dramatic and allegorical model to the novel form?

One point worth noting is the extent to which Dickens has actually preserved simplicity, while working towards a very complex model of the self within the world. In examining the story of *Great Expectations* we have found a 'fairy-tale' quality deriving in part from the action but also from the characters in the book. Idiosyncratic and original as they are, they have clearly recognisable functions or roles: stepmother, fairy godmother, companion, beloved and so on. They are distinguished physically and by their attributes. There is no duplication or redundancy: only one person performs each role, and where we might feel tempted to group characters together by their functions, what we find is that they must on the contrary be distinguished – for example, there is no confusing Biddy and Estella, though Pip at various times has thoughts of marriage with both of them. In effect, structures of comparison are built up, precisely to allow for contrast to appear.

Multiplication and differentiation of characters, then, permit increasing cross-reference, and lead towards complexity though by simple means. Perhaps the greatest development from *David Copperfield* is in the concentration of both these, apparently antithetical, processes, through the device of making Pip more *aware* of the possibility of comparison than David was, both now as he narrates the story and then while he was embroiled in it. Pip's ghostly apprehensions and half-glimpsed perceptions and anxieties are particularly effective in generating such processes of understanding (in him and in us) without obtruding an awkward structure of explication into the narrative to strain probability. It is imaginative not rigorously intellectual understanding that is called for – a process, not a rigid construct: deconstruction, not clinical analysis.

In keeping with this fluid and responsive understanding (undermining 'expectations'), any 'structures of characterisation' are continually challenged by the quirky liveliness of the characters themselves. We might adapt a moment from the novel – a moment not apparently concerned with character – as a kind of image or paradigm of this challenge of experience. Here Pip returns to the marshes carrying a file and a pork pie for the convict, his conscience burdened and his perceptions both heightened and distorted by guilty fear. He describes this experience vividly yet oddly, as a sequence of blind encounters followed by recognition (however distorted); all sending him back towards Magwitch and the scene of his first guilt. The active and passive roles are disconcertingly reversed in Pip's progress, for as he hurries along he feels as if the world is running at him. So in this passage our protagonist is exposed. He is turned from adventurer to quarry, observer to the object of observation. He is the guilty party: it is he who becomes known:

> On every rail and gate, wet lay clammy; and the marsh-mist was so thick, that the wooden finger on the post directing people to our village – a direction which they never accepted, for they never came there – was invisible to me until I was quite close under it. Then, as I looked up at it, while it dripped, it seemed to my oppressed conscience like a phantom devoting me to the Hulks.
>
> The mist was heavier yet when I got out upon the marshes, so that instead of my running at everything, everything seemed to run at me. This was very disagreeable to a guilty mind. The gates and dykes came bursting through the mist, as if they cried as plainly as could be, 'A boy with Somebody-else's pork pie! Stop him!' (Ch. 3, p. 48)

Like the physical world running at Pip here, characters start up in the novel text, seemingly mysterious, even when they carry clear signs; they offer him pointers back towards his origins in poverty at the forge; they stir his sense of guilt, deriving from this first action which binds him into criminal association with Magwitch. Characters crop up out of the 'mist' of his (and our) confusion and ignorance, and their effect is as often comical as frightful.

The initial impact of every character is a strong sense of otherness: they are, above all, strange; but Pip's pattern of development involves recognising something within these strange beings, and sensing a kind of kinship with them. In his sense – in our sense – of them, there is a transition from the 'other' to the 'known', from objectification to identification, from observation to understanding. (Pip's development in this is more sophisticated than David Copperfield's, and closer to that of the reader in both works.) Thus in Pip's experience (and in ours) the pale young gentleman springs inexplicably out of nowhere as an assailant, but becomes Herbert Pocket, room-mate, exemplar, friend, patron and protégé; someone very close to Pip himself. And so, in some sense, it is with every other character: not just the good, but the bad; warnings as well as examples, grotesque, caricatured, shadowy, lurid. Magwitch is the most striking example of this 'recognition pattern', transforming the terrifying 'other' into human 'kin', and so enlarging Pip's own inner being: his moral and imaginative core. Only after recognising Magwitch as his benefactor can Pip truly begin to see the force of an even older bond of kinship with Joe Gargery, that 'gentle Christian man' who is the best exemplar of humanity. Magwitch and Joe might seem the extremes of 'other' and 'kin', bad and good, unacceptable and acknowledged, but in fact Pip has to learn to acknowledge them both: starting, as we see, with the less likely. The capacity to accept both Magwitch and Joe is the mark of mature human values; and in each case Pip's recognition is a reciprocation of the other man's feeling: they grow, not more *like*, but *closer* to each other, and the process establishes the sense of shared humanity, rising above individual personality.

A greater test than Magwitch or Joe, however, comes with the character of Orlick: a figure of uncanny power, so tricky to deal with (socially for Pip, narratologically for the novel, imaginatively for the reader) that he might almost have been put in to *Great Expectations* for the very purpose of trying our understanding and proving the rule. Can Pip come to terms with him? What does he mean for Pip; what does he do? How does he function in the novel and affect our attempt to comprehend the interrelationship of the individual with the world? In his abrupt introduction, and even stranger disappearance from the novel, Orlick both raises such questions and allows them to remain unanswered if need be: areas of mystery surrounding the darkness in Pip's life. There is some affinity between the relationship of Pip with Orlick and Estella's with Bentley Drummle. Both Pip and Estella exhibit a certain fascination with destructive violence: Pip's evidently involuntary, Estella's recklessly self-willed. Both suffer, but survive; only after their experience of such aggression can they meet in peace together.

There is, strange as it may seem, a point of correspondence between Orlick and Estella in relation to Pip. Estella is of course quite unlike Orlick in every way – except that the response she arouses in Pip is extreme, beyond measure, explanation, or control. If Orlick inspires loathing, she excites desire. For Pip she represents the absolute 'other', the unattainable; yet she is 'part of his existence' by his own confession. In Chapter 29 Pip distils the paradox of the novel, reaching the height of objectivity and the depths of subjective experience at the same time, in writing the account of his love:

The unqualified truth is, that when I loved Estella with the love of a man, I loved her simply because I found her irresistible. Once for all; I knew to my sorrow, often and often, if not always, that I loved her against reason, against promise, against peace, against hope, against happiness, against all discouragement that could be. Once for all, I loved her none the less because I knew it, and it had no more influence in restraining me, than if I had devoutly believed her to be human perfection. (Ch. 29, pp. 253-4)

(It is intriguing to note that straight after this avowal the narrative continues with a wholly unexpected encounter with Dolge Orlick, transported to the position of porter at Miss Havisham's door.)

The style and tone of Pip's declaration of love, astonishing and touching as they are, grow credibly from qualities present in him from the very beginning of the novel. Dickens both characterises Pip and equips him as a narrator by endowing him with a verbal precision to match his acute perceptions: two qualifications for the storyteller, held in ironical (and psychologically plausible, and narratologically necessary) balance against his ignorance and mis-understanding. It is thanks to Pip's rather formal style, dispassion-ate clarity of vision and succinct, self-ironising tone that we are taught how to read *Great Expectations*: what to notice, what to enjoy, and how to divide our attention and sympathies between Pip then, Pip now and Pip's world. From Pip's (quasi-scriptural) genealogical self-introduction, through the rude interruption of the convict, and on to Pip's sister and Joe Gargery at the forge, one novelistic mode succeeds another, bringing rapid changes of mood and readerly expectation, from formal history to gothic horror, then fable. Throughout these shifts, however, we hear the ingenuous voice of Pip, prompting in us something of his own curiosity and delicious disquiet. So Dickens promotes something beyond passivity and credulity in the audience: the beginnings of a process beyond fiction; the critical recognition of character, the registration of significance and the sense of Pip's complex role in this.

At the start of the text Pip sets out to tell us his name and ancestry, but he cannot get either quite right. Instead of 'authority', we are given invention, adaptation and imagination. The tomb-stone inscription engraved in stone does not predicate the whole text, but feeds 'unreasonably' into Pip's 'first fancies' (Chapter 1). One kind of 'character' (the written letter) turns into another (imaginatively alive) – through the medium of Pip's mind:

> As I never saw my father or my mother, and never saw any likeness of either of them (for their days were long before the days of photographs), my first fancies regarding what they were like, were unreasonably derived from their tombstones. The shape of the letters on my father's gave me an odd idea that he was a square, stout, dark man, with curly black hair. From the character and turn of the inscription '*Also Georgiana Wife of the Above*', I drew a childish conclusion that my mother was freckled and sickly. (Ch. 1, p. 35).

This surprisingly modernistic (punning on the written text as a superimposed metafiction, and 'conclusions' drawn like sketches) and comical turn to the reflections of the orphan in the graveyard is disruptive to the *tone* of the scene. A pathetic vignette turns to a comic sketch. The disturbance affects the *action*. A 'terrible voice' interrupts Pip's narrative monologue. A 'fearful' man intrudes: as Dickens has it, 'A fearful man, all in coarse grey, with a great iron on his leg' (Ch. 1, p. 36); no verb; simply the fact; 'fearful' to Pip but perhaps (beyond the understanding of the child) himself full of fear too. This man, the paragraph goes on to show, is an object of horror: the passive subject of a great string of verbs, giving the effect of creation animated against him, and reducing him to a pitiable state:

> A fearful man, all in coarse grey, with a great iron on his leg. A man with no hat, and with broken shoes, and with an old rag tied round his head. A man who had been soaked in water, and smothered in mud, and lamed by stones, and cut by flints, and stung by nettles, and torn by briars; who limped, and shivered, and glared, and growled; and whose teeth chattered in his head as he seized me by the chin. (Ch. 1, p. 36)

Strange and terrible is the creature thus described, a thing almost elemental, beast rather than man. And this is very important. The monstrous shock of Magwitch's first appearance inscribes his significance for Pip: an indelible nightmare, through his long absence from Pip's experience and from the text. Yet here in the first glimpse of the convict, half-obscured by horror, we can already see the qualities which Pip will eventually recognise, uniting them as fellow human beings. The first clue is that ambiguous adjective 'fearful', hinting at an emotion common to boy and man. Then, like the 'small bundle of shivers' growing afraid, the convict 'shivered' too. While *he* eats ravenously, 'licking his lips', he calls *Pip* 'You young dog'; then Pip, when he brings the stolen food (Chapter 3), gives an extended comparison between the convict's way of eating and 'a large dog of ours' (p. 50). Convict and boy are both hunted, and both haunted too by the second man; Magwitch is condemned and Pip feels implicated in his guilt.

Human emotion, appetite, and guilt, are all powerful bonds between Pip and the convict. Magwitch also, rather surprisingly, displays an imaginative invention (and psychological penetration) in this scene, which gives him a kind of affinity with our story-teller. His creation of 'That young man' who will punish any failing in the boy works with Pip's fears to dramatic effect, much as Pip's lies after seeing Satis House are to work with his sister's fantasies. Nor does the inventiveness stop here: story after story is told by different characters in *Great Expectations*, some 'true', others refracted by selfishness, as in Mrs Joe's version of her life story compared with Joe's. Together all these tales assail the boundaries of 'truth', offering different kinds of revelation, some unwitting, and the cumulative effect is to extend our understanding of the possibilities of first-person narrative as a form, and hence our responsiveness to the different aspects of Pip's story.

The introduction of Magwitch in Chapters 1, 3 and 5 alternates with that of Mr and Mrs Joe Gargery and their circle. The contrast adds force to both nightmare and childhood memories. We see how Pip's world is structured, physically, socially and morally in terms of inside and out (all the more poignant since the first 'inner space' is that of the grave – to which the whole world, and life itself, is 'outside': perhaps, like the escaped convict). When Miss Havisham beckons Pip to Satis House, this merely adds another closely comparable layer to the structure. Pip finds an 'inner sanctum' to which he longs to belong – but some of his most painful moments are those in the passages and at the door, where Estella (and much later, disconcertingly, Orlick) makes him very conscious of his status as an outsider, suffered merely to call and visit.

The association between character and place, even before physical description or speech, lays stress first on the social position, and only then on individualising characteristics, of figures in Pip's world. The two are often in conflict, so that personal oddity challenges convention. Bringing them into equilibrium is an achievement both of social maturity and personal development for Pip, as a new set of moral and emotional values displaces the old markers. He comes to know them as he does himself. So we find three structures of characterisation in the novel: social, personal and the scale of relationship to Pip. The three are interwoven, but also surprisingly independent, and this gives rise to the sustained sense of wonder which is the novel's chief distinction, and defiance of the bleak graveyard promise of the opening.

The contest of entity with correspondence in characterisation, or selfhood versus relation-to-Pip, is complex and hard to disentangle. What could be more unlike than the string of those 'adopting' or 'adopted by' Pip: Magwitch, Joe, Pumblechook, Herbert Pocket, Jaggers, Wemmick, the Avenger in Boots – to stick to male characters, and to say nothing of those (equally significant) who set him at defiance: Orlick, or Trabb's boy, or Bentley Drummle? We might hope to go more steadily through the female characters: there are fewer of them, and their relations with Pip might seem more limited. Yet two complications soon emerge. We need to tackle the extreme case of Estella: is she most like, or most unlike Pip, closest, or furthest from him? Then too we notice the extraordinary density of correspondences between Estella and the other female characters (the other male figures also, of course) – quite apart from, or better, in addition to, the links and strains with Pip. Any critical grouping of characters, with or without Pip himself, runs across the problem of criss-crossing lines of likeness and difference, and the interactions of their wishes and wills, terror, guilt and desire.

The first woman mentioned in the text is Mrs Joe Gargery, an 'authority' held in syntactic equivalence with the tombstone: 'I give Pirrip as my father's family name, on the authority of his tombstone and my sister' (Ch. 1, p. 35). The second is her mother (and Pip's), buried beneath that slab. Her inscription, 'Also

Georgiana', exactly epitomises her (evidently mortal) *dependency*, as wife, mother, fellow-corpse, briefly summoned up in Pip's fancy as 'freckled and sickly' (*ibid.*). Against this inscribed fate, the redoubtable Mrs Joe's 'authority' has a different force, as the will to resist annihilation – though she too will in turn be brought low, and die. The absent mother and inadequate sister dramatise the want of love for Pip: this is their direct bearing on him. But in themselves, especially when their fortunes are compared, they demonstrate (by default) something more: the vital human balance of weakness and strength, timidity and desire, whose disequilibrium makes life, apparently, impossible. Pip's own version of this 'universal struggle' involves both his accommodation to good fortune and its reversal, and also the poise with which he surveys and relates his history. Active and passive are forces in perception and composition as they are in primary experience. Pip's text starts with a tombstone but proceeds as a vivid autobiography; no inscription of fate.

Mrs Joe, like her mother, is introduced through her relationship to others: 'my sister – Mrs Joe Gargery, who married the blacksmith' (Ch. 1, p. 35). We never know her by any other name. Her age is also given in relative terms, as 'more than twenty years older than I' (Ch. 2, p. 39). Such facts place her publicly. She herself seems to have contributed to this process, and even internalised it (a point Dickens makes partly through the economical method of grammatical compression): 'My sister, Mrs Joe Gargery, was more than twenty years older than I, and *had established a great reputation with herself and the neighbours* because she had brought me up "by hand" ' (*ibid. – my italics*). Even her appearance is approached through a public judgement, and shown to have a bearing on her social position: 'She was not a good-looking woman, my sister; and I had a general impression that she must have made Joe Gargery marry her by hand' (*ibid.*). She and Joe are characterised by strength and weakness, both physical and temperamental – though these characteristics are in fact ambivalent in both of them – neither of them neatly meeting nor fully reversing our stereotypes of gender. Comically reductive as the description of Mrs Joe is, its effect is not to fix but to unsettle the disposition of determination as an aspect of character. The old joke of the harpy and the henpecked husband does not fully explain the Gargerys' relationship, for Joe, 'a sort of Hercules in strength, and also in weakness' (Ch. 2, p. 40) has resources in reserve while Mrs Joe's ferocity is so exaggerated that we must suspect it expresses need, rather than simple tyranny. Black and red are her colours (like the 'angry' landscape of evening over the marshes); 'coarse', 'strong', and 'powerful' are the adjectives that dominate her description. But together with these features comes something more telling: 'She was tall and bony, and almost always wore a coarse apron, fastened over her figure behind with two loops, and having a square impregnable bib in front, that was stuck full of pins and needles' (*ibid.*). This warlike garment could be seen as weapon or defence: Mrs Joe is 'impregnable' only if she is attacked (and not then, in fact, as we are to find out – the bib protects her front, but she is struck from behind); there is an air of the martyr about those pins and needles. While she wields a stick, Mrs Joe talks of herself as a slave. Her fate is worse than that, when she is battered into submission. 'However,' Pip tells us with chilling composure, 'her temper was greatly improved, and she was patient' (Ch. 16, p. 150). She is also now immobile, unintelligible, unable to see properly, suffers a 'tremulous uncertainty of the action of all her limbs' and 'would often put her hands to her head, and would then remain for about a week at a time in some gloomy aberration of mind' (Chapter 16). When, finally, she succeeds in having Orlick brought in, Pip is 'disappointed' by her improved temper:

> She watched his countenance as if she were particularly wishful to be assured that he took kindly to his reception, she showed every possible desire to conciliate him, and there was an air of humble propitiation in all she did, such as I have seen pervade the bearing of a child towards a hard master. (Ch. 16, p. 151)

Why is this behaviour disturbing, both to Pip and Orlick? So complete a submission effectively overturns the balance of power by destroying the pattern of hostility itself. Instead of the bully beaten, we see a helpless victim: one who, like the child within the adult, has always been there within Mrs Joe. Chapter 15, immediately before this attack, showed her first provoking the fight at the forge, then dropping insensible at the window. That episode and this are evidently related: but how? Pip assumes that the earlier beating prompted Orlick's revenge, but why does Mrs Joe respond as she does? No direct answer is given. We can only infer the reason gradually and indirectly, by piecing together all the evidence we have already had about Mrs Joe's complex nature and circumstances, and by drawing analogies with other cases in the novel of fury and repression, destructive desire and the oblique effects of suffering. In other words, the puzzle so bluntly posed by Mrs Joe's wretched, but apparently incidental, case acts as a clue to something better hidden, but present, within Pip himself.

It is not until the struggle with Orlick at the lime kilns that Pip will have enough distance from his early life to analyse the tangle of resentment between himself and Orlick and his sister, and to understand how penetrating (and how curiously public and mutual) was the sense of his own guilt in this action, in which he played apparently so little part. At that stage (Chapter 53), the confrontation will bring out the relationship between two grudges held by Orlick: over Mrs Joe, and with Miss Havisham; in both cases, Pip stood in his way. Again, it is Pip who is at the centre – no matter who would appear to be the dramatis personae of the action – and Orlick is his dark shadow. But we can find clues before Orlick's denunciation, anticipating and perhaps endorsing his shocking accusations – which are themselves a voice for Pip's own self-reproach. Miss Havisham is linked to Pip through plot and theme in many ways, and only rather incidentally through Orlick. But the Orlick connection helps bring out that one of the ways in which she is bound up with him also involves Pip's sister. Like Mrs Joe, Miss Havisham tyrannises over Pip's early years, although her influence lasts longer. At first the two women seem to offer alternative dispensations for the child: in the forge or at Satis House. But it is as Estella's guardian, not Pip's, and in apposition to Magwitch through her function as sponsor, that Miss Havisham plays her part in the plot. Thematically, she resembles the convict, ambitious for revenge, and using her ward as a human instrument of her will. Nevertheless, despite her class distinction and her different role, Miss Havisham has links too with Mrs Joe, a character she never meets but who, like her, suffers a crippling resentment deriving from familial and sexual betrayal: Miss Havisham is affianced then abandoned through the agency of her half-brother; Mrs Joe is married out of pity for her little brother's plight. The greater the strain in recognising this affinity, paradoxically, the more apparent it becomes that both characters, from their different positions and in their different ways, offer analogies too for something present in Pip himself: the bitterness binding social inferiority with sexual frustration.

It is the social signals of Miss Havisham's catastrophe that strike Pip first, although they rapidly come to function as symbols of personal disgrace and despair. So the novel recognises demonstrable difference before intuited affinity (Pip has just met Estella, and experienced her scorn for the first time, which he finds 'very uncomfortable'). Miss Havisham is a 'fine lady', 'the strangest lady I have ever seen, or shall ever see', a 'withered' bride, 'ghastly waxwork' and 'skeleton' before she speaks, and it is long indeed before she seems to Pip a fellow human being.

Structurally and thematically, the introduction of Miss Havisham into the text (Chapter 8) parallels the irruption of Magwitch (Chapter 1), and though it is superficially very different, this 'second start' is carefully designed to have equal imaginative weight. An extended approach to the moment begins in the previous weekly part (Chapter 7), and builds up through Pip's journey to Satis House, his encounter with Estella and the progress through gate and courtyard, door, passages, staircase and 'at last' the dressing-room door (Ch. 8, p. 86). What Pip sees inside is 'a pretty large room', 'well lighted', with grand furniture strange to the country boy. Only then does he notice the 'fine lady', an object as prodigious as her surroundings. His catalogue of her effects, from pose to costume, textures, colour, ornaments and the things scattered in confusion about her, is both orderly and impressionistic. The perceptions of the moment merge with a narrative design; Pip is careful to report, 'It was not in the first few moments that I saw all these things, though I saw more of them in the first moments than might be supposed' (Ch. 8, p. 87). Here two textual processes, two temporal locations and two characters are held in balance, competing for our attention, and at the same time enabling us to pass from one to the other. The description, the moment and Miss Havisham stand as solid items of the story; but through the same passage, Pip's processes of perception and registration, his awareness of the time that has now passed and of what that means for him, and above all our sense of Pip as the presence through whom Miss Havisham is made available to us, direct the narrative. Miss Havisham has frozen time, but she personifies the processes of mortality; Pip, from bewildered boy to wondering narrator, exemplifies another approach to experience, and the two comment on each other.

There are three paragraphs presenting Miss Havisham: they grow in length as Pip's focal distance decreases, so that his object of vision is actually absorbed in his contemplation, and he, rather than she, becomes the centre of his experience. The first paragraph is curiously impersonal; the second is dominated by the pronoun 'she' and possessive 'her'; the third reiterates 'I saw' (five times) and 'Once, I had been taken to see' (twice). Pip's past and Miss Havisham's are somehow brought together through that movement inwards and back. Eventually, the pitiful figure and wondering spectator seem to share a nervous system: 'Now, waxwork and skeleton seemed to have dark eyes that moved and looked at me. I should have cried out, if I could' (Ch. 8, p. 87). In fact it is not Pip but Miss Havisham who speaks, uttering the first of a series of spare questions and abrupt commands, challenging a response inconceivable in the child, and imperiously foreshortening his development by demands that he answer her adult pain. Like Mrs Joe, she centres herself in the text, demonstrating martyrdom:

'What do I touch?'
  'Your heart.'
  'Broken!'
  She uttered the word with an eager look and with strong emphasis, and with a weird smile that had a kind of boast in it. (Ch. 8, p. 88)

When Pip declines to 'play, play, play!' at her bidding, she is touched by his plea of the strange and fine and melancholy place, and the interaction of the strange and familiar proceeds further between them through a lilting refrain of words and looks, repeated and exchanged:

> I stopped, fearing I might say too much, or had already said it, and we took another look at each other.
> Before she spoke again, she turned her eyes from me, and looked at the dress she wore, and at the dressing-table, and finally at herself in the looking-glass.
> 'So new to him,' she muttered, 'so old to me; so strange to him, so familiar to me; so melancholy to both of us! Call Estella.'
> As she was still looking at the reflection of herself, I thought she was still talking to herself, and kept quiet.
> 'Call Estella,' she repeated, flashing a look at me, 'You can do that. Call Estella. At the door.' (Ch. 8, p. 89)

Estella's entry does nothing to disperse the tension of the scene, but she does displace Miss Havisham as the centre of interest, and this initiates the painful and wayward development in Pip of love, which is perhaps his own counterpart to Miss Havisham's preoccupation with the looking-glass: the opportunity for metaphorical reflection, doubling and distancing his 'self' into two distinct but inseparable parts. Meanwhile, Miss Havisham lapses into watchful silence: as if throughout this mysterious episode there is the same quantity of psychic life, but differently distributed amongst the three participants. The dialogue, action and focus of the scene move rhythmically, linking and interweaving the actors, and expressing an imaginative energy which does not seem to derive from or be bound by the old conventions of character. An exhausting, mesmeric expectancy urges the accumulated frustrations of the past (principally Miss Havisham's, though not exclusively) into action upon the future (principally Estella's and Pip's). The air of inevitability makes even Miss Havisham's effort of will strangely impersonal: she, no less than Estella and Pip, is reduced to the status of an object of the ritualised process; and *her* physical collapse obliquely expresses something about *Pip's* surrender:

> 'You shall go soon,' said Miss Havisham, aloud. 'Play the game out.'
> Saving for the one weird smile at first, I should have felt almost sure

that Miss Havisham's face could not smile. It had dropped into a watchful and brooding expression – most likely when all things about her had become transfixed – and it looked as if nothing could ever lift it up again. Her chest had dropped, so that she spoke low, and with a dead lull upon her; altogether, she had the appearance of having dropped, body and soul, within and without, under the weight of a crushing blow.

I played the game to an end with Estella, and she beggared me. She threw the cards down on the table when she had won them all, as if she despised them for having been won of me. (Ch. 8, p. 91)

Estella too, for all her haughty demeanour, is caught up in this process which subordinates character: her very pride is fostered to that end. Her contempt of Pip and delight in his tears come to order: they are no more personal than his 'smart without a name'. And Pip's response extends the impersonality of the forces at play when he explains this moment by referring to a character not present: Estella humiliates him, and he writes, 'My sister's bringing up had made me sensitive.' Again, figures merge into each other in the garden of Satis House, when Pip first fancies then actually sees Estella walking away from him, and then he imagines another vision:

A figure all in yellow white, with but one shoe to the feet; and it hung so, that I could see that the faded trimmings of the dress were like earthy paper, and that the face was Miss Havisham's, with a movement going over the whole countenance as if she were trying to call to me. (Ch. 8, p. 94)

This ghoulish apparition has several functions: to heighten the drama of the episode, and convey Pip's sensitivity and excitement; to confirm and extend the impressions we already have of Miss Havisham as a living corpse; and to urge the narrative on towards the consummation of that end. Pip's vision here anticipates Miss Havisham's own relish in her future state, detailed to the relatives who will 'come to feast' upon her (Ch. 11, p. 116). But it is interesting that she is not in fact hanged, nor laid out quite as she foresees: expectations even of that great event are slightly awry – and this expresses ironically the fallibility of the will, which Miss Havisham represents, corresponding to the helplessness of Pip's wishes, in the novel.

Pip's first notions of gentility come from Satis House and are conditioned by Miss Havisham. The fervency of his aspirations is matched by the horror of the spectacle: desire, fear and guilt are bound up together. Innocence has no place here: Pip is used to torment the relatives, who for their part aggravate the sense of his exclusion. So do Estella and Miss Havisham herself, the gentleman with the scented hands (Jaggers), and even the 'pale young gentleman' in the garden. This young man's challenge, ' "Who let *you* in?" ' (Ch. 11, p. 119) epitomises what Pip takes to be the world's stance. His answer, ' "Miss Estella" ', is deeply ironic, for she embodies rejection, the unattainable desire.

Candlelight and darkness, fire and chill, jewels and decay, robes half shed, the 'work' of playing at cards, express the contradictions of this world in physical terms. But its values are imaginative, not material, to Pip: that is why they are most forcefully conveyed through the figures of the witch and the fairy, the abandoned and the unreachable bride. These fairy-tale constructs grow more complicated, however, as Pip grows up; and his gradual understanding of the complexities of the world, whether fine or homely, goes together with a developing perception of the conflicts between, and within, Miss Havisham and Estella. The girl plays out too well her guardian's vengeful resolve. The balance of power and need shifts between them. Miss Havisham changes from the gloating mistress of her own decay to 'a ghastly stare of pity and remorse' (Ch. 44, p. 378). Once falsely assumed to be Pip's benefactress, eventually she agrees to do good on his behalf secretly for Herbert Pocket. At last she is destroyed, not by darkness, but 'a great flaming light' (Ch. 49, p. 414), and Pip falls with her, struggling like an enemy, to save her as a friend. Her white dress is reduced to black tinder, and replaced by bandages. What she feels is remorse, for Estella, for Pip, perhaps for herself: and her end acts upon them, and not simply her. Even the annihilation of character has a force beyond the individual personality.

In Pip's last encounter with Miss Havisham, as in his first, the episode demonstrates through character, action and scene, forces which derive from a deeper psychological (and narrative) point than this moment, and have repercussions beyond it: like an earthquake or a volcanic explosion. Nor are these the only instances of this deep imaginative power working obliquely through the text. Pip's narrative depends heavily on the energy of episodes and characters which might appear to be only tangentially related to him, but which in effect bring his story to its full expression. Character is an element in this process because it focuses imaginative power in complex ways. But it is a force which gives way to something beyond personality in the narrative: the sense of what runs through these disparate and complicated individuals, and constitutes their common humanity. Pip is central to this because of his narrative function as well as his position in the story: it is the gathering and telling of experience which opens it, and him, to us. Confrontation, perception and accommodation or rejection occur between characters, causing the generation and release of imaginative energy, which is not necessarily specific to one or other but may move between them – and even between episodes. A good example occurs in Chapter 38 when Pip accompanies Estella (now a lady in London) to Satis House at Miss Havisham's behest.

This scene constitutes a crisis for each of the three individuals involved: a separate though contingent catastrophe for Pip and Miss Havisham, and predicament for Estella. The focus is on the encounter between these two, protectress and ward. Yet even this serves a function in the narrative as a whole which has less to do with them than with Pip: a point which Dickens makes clearly, but not explicitly, through structure – and daringly over a series of no less than three weekly parts. To judge the force of character in this episode we have to take account of narrative structure, just as much as appearance, actions and dialogue within the scene: there is a more extensive subtext than the participants could know at the time.

Our first clue comes before Chapter 38, when the previous part closes on Pip's anticipation of 'a great event in my life' (the one which is to be narrated in Chapter 39 with the return of Magwitch), but explicitly turns away temporarily to 'give one chapter to Estella' (Ch. 37, p. 318). This creates an interesting counterpoint between crucial and extensive elements in the narrative, interlocking different periods of time, moving at disparate pace and allowing for different kinds of imaginative weight to co-exist. And there is a further irony: for it will emerge in due course that the 'great event' which here competes with Estella for Pip's narrative attention is not a sudden intrusion, but the culmination of a development begun even before Estella entered his life.

Pip opens Chapter 38 as a wandering spirit, haunting the house in Richmond where Estella lives. She makes use of him to torment her other suitors, and her behaviour, as well as his feelings, recalls the old days at Satis House: 'she habitually reverted to that tone which expressed that our association was forced upon us' (Ch. 38, p. 319), though there are moments 'when she would come to a sudden check in this tone and in all her many tones, and would seem to pity me' (*ibid.*). Pip's devotion, Estella's disdain and the hints too of contrary tendencies, all make it appropriate that their relationship should be returned to Satis House and played out as before in Miss Havisham's presence there; we understand 'the condition of [their] going', and how one 'must obey' (Ch. 38, p. 320) – this is all the preparation needed to imbue the occasion with all the old inevitability of Pip's first experience 'up town'.

Miss Havisham is 'positively dreadful' in her attentions to Estella and her attitude to Pip, and the 'energy of her looks and embraces' (*ibid.*) no less than the 'devouring' of her ward and 'searching' of Pip all direct attention beneath the surface of the scene to the passions just below it. While Miss Havisham pierces Pip and Estella with her glances, he (through the narrative) penetrates her, in a way which recalls that early interchange between them through the medium of the looking-glass, and expresses the psychic energy of interaction, rather than individual will:

> From Estella she looked at me, with a searching glance that seemed to pry into my heart and probe its wounds. 'How does she use you, Pip; how does she use you?' she asked me again, with her witch-like eagerness, even in Estella's hearing. (*ibid.*)

It is a spectacle that Pip thinks he can read: 'I saw in this', he repeats, time after time, 'I saw in this, the distinct shadow of the darkened and unhealthy house in which her life was hidden from the sun' (Ch. 38, p. 321). He is both right and wrong: seeing both less and more than Miss Havisham does; for while he is mistaken in the idea (soon to be corrected) that she has his life in charge as she has Estella's, Pip understands better than Miss Havisham how diseased her affections have become. That is what this scene is to bring home; and the 'sharp words' between Estella and her guardian will give voice to a resentment, pride and resistance that are to underlie the following episode also – with its different actors – when Pip encounters Magwitch.

This structural perspective helps explain the curiously outspoken quality of this scene, which is without parallel in the relations of Estella and the woman she here (and here only) calls 'Mother by adoption'. Miss Havisham attacks her indifference, coldness, ingratitude and demands 'Love', in a word. Estella, 'only moving her eyes' (in an extension of that ballet of looks with which the encounter began), stands easily, cool, at the great chimney-piece, and sets out in phrases as brusque and measured as her mentor's the process which has led her to this. While Miss Havisham exclaims, moans and shrieks, Estella relentlessly puts it to her, in a series of questions, whether she has not brought about the very state of affairs she now laments. Their difference of physical attitude literally expresses an emotional, and moral, gulf, which Estella's 'calm wonder' paradoxically underlines.

Our interest in this coolness centres on the personality it seems both to mask and expose: we wonder at Estella's control, and at the forces which have brought her to this. But her summary makes a point in curiously dispassionate terms, which allow us, if we will, to recall this moment in the following scene – a scene of very different and less analytical temper – and to explore its application there. For Estella speaks in abstract terms that disavow personality and substitute alien will: ' "So," said Estella, "I must be taken as I have been made. The success is not mine, the failure is not mine, but the two together make me" ' (Ch. 38, p. 324). It is the retort Pip does not make, but might have done, to his 'maker' Magwitch, when Magwitch reveals himself in Chapter 39 as his 'second father'.

At that point, in a different location, and with Pip the only common actor, we can see that the moral issues and emotional forces raised between Miss Havisham and Estella in Chapter 38 have a bearing beyond their individual characters, and play a part in educating Pip inwardly for his own imminent trial of love: love not as erotic passion, but as need which cannot be ignored.

The return of Magwitch (Chapter 39) would seem to shift the axis of the narrative, but within six chapters Pip is back at Satis House, confronting Miss Havisham and Estella once again: impelled by the need to relate the two strands of his worldly and emotional fortune, which so suddenly have been apparently divorced. Chapter 44 contributes nothing to the plot (except most secretively in the mention of Estella's knitting fingers, which are to link her in Pip's mind with her unknown mother) although it has a narrative function in clarifying for the reader the outlines of a story stretched over many weekly parts and monthly numbers since its opening. But this is not the chief purpose of the episode; rather, that lies in what it shows us of Pip, both 'directly' through his own self-analysis, and obliquely through the opportunity to compare him with the other two participants. Yet again, assembled in the same location, and with the familiar tension between looks and words, costumes, gestures, demonstrative drama and a subtext of suppression, we see the interlocking of 'story' and 'character' and feel how arbitrary and clumsy such concepts may be.

The outcome of the interview is Pip's avowal to Estella of his unchangeable feeling for her. Interestingly, this is not a conventional declaration of love – according to the moral, emotional and plot expectations of the nineteenth-century novel, growing between two people and issuing in marriage – but a thoroughly unconventional claim of pervasive influence, amounting to identity, and associated with a series of non-human aspects of life. Pip's speech may recall Catherine's 'I am Heathcliff' speech in *Wuthering Heights*, but it might be more clearly read as a striking anticipation of what D. H. Lawrence claimed he wanted to write in *The Rainbow*: that which is 'non-human in humanity' (Letter to Edward Garnet, 5 June 1914). One of these analogues has been judged the epitome of Romanticism, the other prototypical Modernism. Pip's speech has, in fact, traces of both. The sentence rhythms and repetitions mark Pip's words as a romantic utterance, but the substance is essentially analytical, cool and strong – qualities which in themselves endorse the kinship Pip is claiming between the composed Estella and himself:

'You will get me out of your thoughts in a week.'

'Out of my thoughts! You are part of my existence, part of myself. You have been in every line I have ever read, since I first came here, the rough common boy whose poor heart you wounded even then. You have been in every prospect I have ever seen since – on the river, on the sails of the ships, on the marshes, in the clouds, in the light, in the darkness, in the wind, in the woods, in the sea, in the streets. You have been the embodiment of every graceful fancy that my mind has ever become acquainted with. The stones of which the strongest London buildings are made, are not more real, or more impossible to be displaced by your hands, than your presence and influence have been to me, there and everywhere, and will be. Estella, to the last hour of my life, you cannot choose but remain part of my character, part of the little good in me, part of the evil.' (Ch. 44, p. 378)

Dissolving boundaries of space, time and material substance, this is a large claim, but it is not an imperious annexation, because it also sets aside the personal. In effect, Pip displaces 'character', with its associations of property, choice and morality, and substitutes 'existence', 'presence' and 'influence': the very matter of experience.

This declaration, though set apart stylistically by its length, coherence and metaphorical force, nevertheless grows persuasively from the chapter where it stands because Pip's argument articulates the movement of forces which have been operating as a subtext throughout the encounter, and helps to explain the paradoxical sense of disjunction and relevance yoked together. As in our other examples, the tensions and abrupt transitions in the scene illustrate but are not delimited by 'character'. Arbitrary movements from person to person, speech to gesture, naturalism to symbolism, from one narrative strand to another, and between different tones, are compressed in a very short space. The effect is in no way to elide distinctions, but rather to give indirect expression to another level of significance, where these things are related. So within twenty lines of text we move from Pip's attempt to continue his financial assistance to Herbert with the help of Miss Havisham, on to her asking what else he wants, and to Pip's declaration of love and Estella's calm response. Pip's fervency is met by Miss Havisham's distraction on one side and Estella's indifference on the other: everything seems to have nothing to do with anything else; only Estella's fingers, knitting on, give an imagistic hint of continuity throughout. Yet the whole reads, as Pip's subsequent speech illuminates, like a 'part' song: one textual voice after another taking up the theme, answering, echoing and responding, though tentatively, to the idea of love – whether the love of a friend, a protégé, or lover; its force goes beyond such distinctions, to achieve a curious kind of impersonality and prepare for the full force of the declaration we have already examined:

> 'I began the service myself, more than two years ago, without his knowledge, and I don't want to be betrayed. Why I fail in my ability to finish it, I cannot explain. It is part of the secret which is another person's and not mine.'
> She gradually withdrew her eyes from me, and turned them on the fire. After watching it for what appeared in the silence and by the light of the slowly wasting candles to be a long time, she was roused by the collapse of some of the red coals, and looked towards me again – at first, vacantly – then, with a gradually concentrating attention. All this time, Estella knitted on. When Miss Havisham had fixed her attention on me, she said, speaking as if there had been no lapse in our dialogue:
> 'What else?'
> 'Estella,' said I, turning to her now, and trying to command my trembling voice, 'you know I love you. You know that I have loved you long and dearly.'
> She raised her eyes to my face, on being thus addressed, and her fingers plied their work, and she looked at me with an unmoved countenance. I saw that Miss Havisham glanced from me to her, and from her to me. (Ch. 44, p. 375)

Mrs Joe, Miss Havisham and Estella (Biddy might also be explored here) come with the conventional attributes of character in the novel: social, physical, and personal markers, placing them in the world of *Great Expectations*, so that Pip, and we, can take bearings from them. But crosscurrents of reference between them prompt comparison with the way Pip is presented. Specific observations provoke further analysis, going beyond the conventions of novel character as personality, functionary of the plot, exemplar of theme, or even individual vehicle of emotion. Such separate categories are shown as linked, and even shifting in relation to particular figures. Our reading of a sequence of scenes and structural movement featuring these women offers evidence of Dickens's design, control and manipulation to this end not only of statement, but also of suppression, hesitancy and elision. He creates mystery. This challenging procedure can be traced further when we include more groups and individuals. It leads eventually to the questioning of Pip himself, both as 'character' and in relation to the novel in which he exists, and which could be said to exist through him.

Moving from female to male characters merely confirms the sense that all work in two ways through the novel: as themselves, and as illustrations of Pip's central drive to conceive himself as a character. There are some comically obvious examples amongst the minor figures: Pumblechook, that incarnation of snobbery and greed; Wopsle, whose Thespian aspirations give a distorting-mirror image of Pip's desire to climb. Bentley Drummle, Compeyson and Orlick stand as appalling embodiments of desire taken further, into the obscene reaches of violence, perversion and deceit. Far from Pip, no doubt; and yet the scene (Chapter 43) where he and Drummle compete for the fire at the Blue Boar, as each waits to see Estella, demonstrates brilliantly through the social comedy of boorish rivals how easily they may be brought together. Dickens's command of tone in this episode is satirically honed: Drummle's loutish vigour and Pip's better, but vulnerable, nature are heard even in their veiled insults.

> 'Beastly place,' said Drummle. – 'Your part of the country, I think?'
> 'Yes,' I assented. 'I am told it's very like your Shropshire.'
> 'Not in the least like it,' said Drummle.
> Here Mr Drummle looked at his boots, and I looked at mine, and then Mr Drummle looked at my boots, and I looked at his. (Ch. 43, p. 369)

Comedy of an equally open, but very differently directed, sort overlays Pip's dealing with Wemmick, Jaggers's clerk; though there is a shift in tone as they grow more closely embroiled, when Pip begins to know himself, first through his failings as a would-be gentleman and then on the return of Magwitch. Dickens's handling of Wemmick is fascinating, for he grows in subtlety and depth in proportion to Pip's need of him and capacity to value him. Though less fully presented, Jaggers too develops as a character in a similar way. Eventually Pip takes a quasi-authorial delight (Chapter 51) in bringing about a confrontation and mutual revelation of character between the two, as he explains what he has come to know about Estella's parentage. Here he reveals that the professional masks of clerk and barrister hide depths of 'innocent cheerful playful' gentleness on one side, and responsible loving care on the other: models for the 'gentleman' more appropriate than legalistic polish.

Amongst the male characters, as amongst the women, we can make subdivisions into groups of various kinds, corresponding to their relationship to different aspects of Pip. Criminal versus law-abiding would be one such distinction; humble or 'gentle'; country or city: each of these has clear social signals in the novel, allowing us to fit them with the construct of the central myth of the gentleman, which is both a social and a moral concept. What is most interesting about this kind of ordering is the shifting relations amongst groups, and what emerges is the inadequacy of any simple identification of social with moral value. Wemmick, skirting the law once Magwitch returns from Australia, shows more decency towards Pip than his professional master does. Herbert Pocket is penniless, but unquestionably a true gentleman. He can move easily between London and the country, while Pip is at home in neither. Joe, the humblest figure in the novel, is the best: a 'gentle Christian man' who reorders any conventional scale of values. Yet Pip never becomes a Joe, although he learns to honour him. There is something in Pip – the distinctive quality perhaps – which does not fall within these scales of social and moral good.

Great Expectations shows Pip adopting the idea of 'the gentleman' and attempting to realise it as his own character, only to find that he is working from a false premise, and indeed towards a wrong conclusion. We can chart Pip's development through his relation to other characters: the provocation of Miss Havisham, the lure of Estella, the example of Herbert Pocket, the horror of

Magwitch, the integrity of Joe – all stand as signposts for his progress. The internal complexity of these characters, and the cross-currents between them, prevent such comparisons from becoming too rigid or formulaic. A figure such as Orlick, angry and alien (though fiercely animated by his own sense that any distinction between himself and Pip is unfair: they ought to be equals), provides a serious challenge and important modification to any notion of Pip's character constructed along these lines. But it is the simple narrative shocks – first of sudden riches – then the revelation of their source, that most forcibly expose the schism in Pip between putative gentleman and simple humanity. This divide is also articulated in other ways through the novel: geographically, through the location of his experience in forge or mansion, country or city, even land or water; stylistically, through the modulations of irony, distinguishing pointedly between different levels of knowledge, judgement and understanding; temporally, through the distinctions of childhood and adult experience.

What conditions Pip's progress is first the urgency of ambition, trying to make the future present, then remorse, attempting to bring back the past. The entire narrative is in uneasy poise between its own present and the unreachable moment for which it strives: and this desire, acute in the telling, is the quick of Pip's being. It is also the distillation of the paradox inherent in all narrative: withholding, and telling the story – a game in which the reader's part is to ask to be taken back but then try to hurry on to the end. Pip's character, and each character in the novel as we come to see, is not a fixed identity but rather a force, struggling against displacement, struggling to recuperate an integrity that can never rest in the present. Joe gives the nearest approximation to such wholeness, moral and emotional: he is a figure of Wordsworthian proportions, embodying a lost innocence beyond desire. But even he cannot retain the trustfulness of his early relations with Pip, for whom he once willingly became a child himself, and acted as brother and fellow-sufferer, rather than a father in authority. When Pip eventually returns to Joe at the end of the novel, it is as a visitor from far away; Joe has another little 'Pip' – their love is true, but it has no purchase on the conditions of the world.

6

Reading the Novel

Analysing the narrative elements of story, structure, scene, symbol and character in *Great Expectations* we can construe the novel as a text: that is, not only acknowledge the diversity and penetrative power of its effects, but see that these qualities are created and disposed with an art that stands in a particular relation to its subject. This distinctive stance – the poise of deliberate analysis with unforced loving recognition – is the peculiar property of *Great Expectations*. The balance is what underpins the paradoxes we have noticed throughout our reading: the counterpoint of revelation with secrecy in the story; discrete articulation with integration in structure; drama and subtext in scene; naturalism and arbitrary coding amongst symbols; individuality with reciprocity in character – the whole set of contradictions to which I have annexed the phrase Pip uses in the novel to describe the unwilled mystery of love: 'wonderful inconsistency'. The same schism runs through Pip's character, striving for a wholeness at first misconceived, then seemingly unreachable. And it is through Pip – in the use of the first-person narrator – whose nature is both subject and object, whose being belongs both to now and the past (and whose past was riven with dreams of a fictive future, now lost), that Dickens articulates the 'wonderful inconsistency' of his enterprise integrally with both the form and the substance of his novel. Beyond the question of the narrator lie two further mysteries: the relation of Pip to Dickens himself, and his relation to us, as we read. These reaches of production and reception go beyond any formalism, and may be matters of speculative inference on one side and personal interpretation on the other, but modulating between them is the eye, voice, stance, tone of the first person narrator, both instrument and product of art, initiating us through the intimacies of memory and relation, into the business of what in *David Copperfield* Dickens had called 'The Personal History'.

The shift in terms of the title between the earlier first-person novel and *Great Expectations* is a clue that we are to look through, and not simply at, Pip. His story exemplifies something abstract, which we can trace more widely than his personal case within the world of the novel, but also perhaps read as a comment on Dickens's society – or even the perennial tension between the individual and the world, as each self is imagined and formed.

While examining the minute techniques of first-person narration, therefore, we find Pip opens wider aspects of human experience. His sensory perceptions suggest a substantial world. His voice translates its phenomena into language: the medium of social communication as well as personal expression. His tone and stance indicate a scale of judgement, integrating his individual response with social values. Above all, Pip's memory – including his memory of desires reaching into the future – interlocks with time itself to set down an account that modulates between autobiography and history.

The novel has its own textual span, too, since it takes time to read: something that would have been more obvious when *Great Expectations* was first published in weekly parts. In the process of reading, *longueurs* and anticipation stretch and shrink the pace of the work, structural correspondences create links and echoes; dramatic scenes, periods of reflection, description or intense activity move at different speeds: all these textual effects realise in literary terms the movements of Pip's mind in experience – and have a further relationship both to chronological time and to the social version of it which creates history.

A full demonstration of these correspondences (which we might perhaps try labelling 'wonderful consistency') would obviously require us to trace the entire working of *Great Expectations*, going over again what we have noted already, and adding more in proportion to the full, complex detail and the density of this remarkably economical novel. But we can follow something of the process, observe the use of the first-person narrator and link his relation with the wider implications of the novel by reading one central episode in the context of both corresponding scenes and the shape of the narrative as a whole, especially if we include in this some consideration of the beginning of the novel and its end.

Chapter 39 shows the strengths and subtleties of Pip's first-person narration: immediate and vivid in the limited point of view of the dramatic moment, but ironised and deepened by the extended narrative. The chapter relates the return of Magwitch and marks 'THIS IS THE END OF THE SECOND STAGE OF PIP'S EXPECTATIONS' as an epitaph printed in roman capitals at its foot. The episode is pivotal to the plot of the novel, and therefore invokes comparison with the beginning of Pip's expectations (before he knew it) in Chapter 1, and the close in Chapter 59. Between them these chapters, with Pip as a child, young man and mature adult, chart the history and futility of his 'expectations', stretched out, turned round and redeemed in time. These effects (incomplete until the novel reaches its conclusion) are to some extent anticipated and given resonance by further echoes within this section of the novel (the second volume of the three), and specifically by two episodes: Joe's visit to London in Chapter 27 and Estella's rejection in Chapter 38, immediately before the central episode, of Miss Havisham's claim of 'love'.

Joe's visit is announced by letter: a formal device which interpolates Biddy's tones into Pip's narrative. Her carefully chosen words (so important that Dickens made no fewer than three changes to the text between the 1861 and 1868 editions of the novel, one of which was to separate and capitalise the word 'Servant' in Biddy's formulaic closing signature (p. 498)) alert to us to the sense of decorum which is to be severely tried in this episode, and found wanting in Pip by comparison with Joe's heartfelt dignity.

That split between Pip and Joe is not replicated but it is echoed by the formal division between the young Pip of the moment, locked in his egotism, and the mature narrator who presents him to us. This distinction is explicit in the dry phrasing, curt rhythms and pointed balancing of abstract and simple vocabulary reporting Pip's response to the letter from Biddy:

> I received this letter by post on Monday morning, and therefore its appointment was for next day. Let me confess exactly, with what feelings I looked forward to Joe's coming.
>
> Not with pleasure, though I was bound to him by so many ties; no, with considerable disturbance, some mortification, and a keen sense of incongruity. If I could have kept him away by paying money, I certainly would have paid money. (Ch. 27, p. 240)

The 'keen sense of incongruity' is the key to both comic and pathetic effects throughout the scene. Ironically, however, the furthest reaches of its implications derive not from incongruity but the very opposite. It is the congruence of this episode with that in Chapter 39 that points up the depth of betrayal in both, when Pip not only 'would have paid money' but actually hands over the notes to his unwelcome visitor, and Magwitch passes judgement by burning them.

Before Joe arrives, the boy in top boots makes his appearance in the text, an 'avenging phantom' whose attendance mimics Pip's own upstart posturing in ironic mockery. He is the first (after Biddy, perhaps) of a series of figures introduced or invoked at short intervals throughout this episode – more or less arbitrarily in plot terms – whose function is not narrative but thematic, as they indicate in grotesque, exaggerated, or oblique ways some of the implications of the central relationship between Pip and Joe. These figures offer an indirect commentary on the proceedings. In using them, Dickens relieves some of the pressure on his first-person narrator, for he need not explain, but simply present, this metatext. It is interesting, however, that in Chapter 38 the diversity of figures has narrowed down to the trinity of Pip, Miss Havisham and Estella while by Chapter 39 there are only two, Pip and Magwitch, to 'read'. At that point, the narrative focus is crucial, the angle of vision and interpretation dramatically pointed, while the use of direct action and dialogue challenges the narrative 'frame'.

Pip's dread of Joe's approaching visit appears in his repeated mention of day and time. Then through Pip's ears we hear Joe's large 'state boots' making their clumsy way up the stairs, pausing at each name on the lower floors. Pip's apprehension renders his senses preternaturally acute:

> When at last he stopped outside our door, I could hear his finger tracing
> over the printed letters of my name, and I afterwards distinctly heard him
> breathing in at the keyhole. (Ch. 27, p. 241)

Such physicality is disturbing, and it suggests the intimacy of Pip's
anxiety. Dickens had used these images of the tracing finger and
heavy breathing in *David Copperfield* to present the loathsome
Uriah Heep: for poor Joe to be apprehended in a similar way, the
quantity of distortion involved is indeed revealing.

The scene progresses in these terms – on the surface, a gross
comedy of physical and verbal clumsiness, met with incongruously
formal politeness:

> With his good honest face all glowing and shining, and his hat put down
> on the floor between us, he caught both my hands and worked them
> straight up and down, as if I had been the last-patented Pump.
> 'I am glad to see you, Joe. Give me your hat.' (*ibid.*)

Even in the moment, however, the pain of rejection is felt on both
sides, within the ludicrous. Comedy and pathos are held in
conjunction:

> But Joe, taking it up carefully with both hands, like a bird's nest with
> eggs in it, wouldn't hear of parting with that piece of property, and
> persisted in standing talking over it in a most uncomfortable way. (*ibid.*)

Whose is the bird's nest simile? Not the 'uncomfortable' young
Pip's. Nor is it imputed to Joe – though it comes from his world.
The narrator has found this image in covert tribute to Joe, aligning
himself (and us) with him against the young cuckoo who receives
him so coolly here, having once been fostered by him. Joe's hat,
perched on the chimney-breast, and repeatedly tumbling, only to be
caught and put back, expresses in mute ballet the nervous tension
of the scene. And the chimney-piece will be the place where Estella
stands against Miss Havisham too; then again, the focus
of strain when Pip faces Magwitch in his new rooms as he now
faces Joe.

Joe's small talk relates the history of Wopsle's metropolitan
debut in the part of Hamlet: again, the comical flourishes of the
text give indirect expression to the central concerns, both of this
moment, and the one prefigured here, when the visitor will be

Magwitch. Joe's anecdote is germane to both: ' "Which I meantersay, if the ghost of a man's own father cannot be allowed to claim his attention, what can, Sir?" ' (p. 242).

'A ghost-seeing effect in Joe's own countenance' again brilliantly snatches the dramatic point of view briefly from Pip, as Herbert enters the room. He is the 'ghost', not, in this instance, of Hamlet's father (as Joe or Magwitch might be termed), but of Hamlet (Pip) himself, in that he behaves to Joe with all the courtesy and ease of manner that Pip would like to display but cannot muster. When Herbert leaves, such social graces are abandoned, as Pip 'pettishly' reproaches Joe for his stiffness and Joe responds for 'a single instant' in like kind, with a look. Now Joe brings Pumblechook into the conversation. Like the Avenger in boots, Wopsle, Hamlet's ghost, and Herbert, Pumblechook is a 'reflector' both on this situation and the forthcoming encounter; for he claims to have been Pip's companion and playfellow – usurping Joe's ancient privilege, and in so doing, anticipating Magwitch's rival claim too. Pip's response here is direct, but it will take him a long time to see its full implications: ' "Nonsense. It was you, Joe" ' (p. 245).

Pumblechook is passed over. He was merely the messenger for Miss Havisham: yet another 'surrogate parent' (and supposed benefactor). She, it appears, has succeeded better than Pumblechook in displacing Joe – literally, for it is she who has caused him to come to London, to carry a message for her – and when Pip hears this his attitude towards the messenger changes accordingly.

At this point Dickens shifts the focus of speaking and narrative voice once again, to express the signal gap between Miss Havisham, Joe and Pip in terms of intentions and interpretation. It is appropriate that in introducing Miss Havisham's name (translated by his phonetic spelling into 'Miss A'), Joe adopts 'an air of legal formality, as if he were making his will': the very air most apt to that lady's preoccupations. In giving Pip Miss Havisham's message, using her words, Joe loses his own textual 'voice'; we shift once more from the young Pip's spontaneous response into the mature narrator's comment:

' "Would you tell him, then," said she, "that which Estella has come home and would be glad to see him."

I felt my face fire up as I looked at Joe. I hope one remote cause of its firing may have been my consciousness that if I had known his errand, I should have given him more encouragement. (Ch. 27, p. 246)

When Joe explains that it was Biddy who persuaded him to deliver Miss Havisham's message in person, the chapter rounds again towards its beginning, and Biddy's letter. Although we have witnessed Joe's visit in Pip's rooms and through Pip's eyes, ears and other wracked senses, Biddy's supervision, even in her absence, 'contains' the scene within the framework of her moral judgement, reinforcing all Joe's unspoken claims on Pip's loyalty. At the close, however, it is Joe himself who speaks out with understanding, tolerance and dignity:

'Pip, dear old chap, life is made of ever so many partings welded together, as I may say, and one man's a blacksmith, and one's a whitesmith, and one's a goldsmith and one's a coppersmith. Divisions among such must come, and must be met as they come. If there's been any fault at all today, it's mine.' (*ibid.*)

'Partings welded together', 'Divisions . . . met as they come': these are positive variants on the 'keen sense of incongruity', resolving paradoxes by accepting their 'wonderful inconsistency'. While Joe blesses Pip and slips away, the narrator moves back (slipping into the pluperfect), as it were to gather this capacity for acceptance in to himself. His acknowledgement asserts Joe's qualities through his own recognition of them: it is a distillation of 'divisions . . . met as they come', 'I had not been mistaken in my fancy that there was a simple dignity in him' (*ibid.*). Meanwhile, Joe 'was gone': it is Pip, not Joe, who is being revealed here; and our last glimpse of him is a remorseful, yet still self-centred one.

The tone of Estella's confrontation with Miss Havisham in Chapter 38 is very different from Joe's with Pip. Instead of painful comedy, 'calm wonder' (p. 324) is the oxymoron epitomising the 'keen sense of incongruity' here. So remote, indeed, are Estella's dignity and feminine poise and Miss Havisham's equally feminine hysteria from the gaucheries of that scene or the rough, assertive masculinity of the following encounter, that they serve to disguise the thematic coherence of the three occasions, and avoid blatant signalling of significance in the text. Nevertheless, Estella's protest voices their common ground, from her own particular angle:

> 'I cannot think,' said Estella, raising her eyes after a silence, 'why you should be so unreasonable when I come to see you after a separation. I have never forgotten your wrongs and their causes. I have never been unfaithful to you or your schooling. I have never shown any weakness that I can charge myself with.'
> 'Would it be weakness to return my love?' exclaimed Miss Havisham. 'But yes, yes, she would call it so!' (Ch. 38, p. 324)

Chapter 38 ends with a paragraph turning away from Estella, and another announcing Pip's impending doom. Two weighty sentences liken the catastrophe to 'the Eastern story' where a great slab is prepared to crush 'the bed of state in the flush of conquest'. The comparison is exotic, erotic and martial yet it is not unapt, both to the foregoing and the coming scene. Although this Arabian Nights simile looks like a diversion, it can be interpreted as a valuable directive sign, helping to link the episodes it punctuates. When Pip's wordly fortunes falter, his emotional fantasies will also be destroyed (his fortunes, his fantasies, but not, of course, his inmost feelings, which will as we shall see be liberated gradually and painfully from their selfish centre). And this work of a moment has been long preparing: 'So, in my case; all the work, near and afar, that tended to the end, had been accomplished; and in an instant the blow was struck, and the roof of my stronghold dropped upon me' (Ch. 38, p. 330).

Chapter 39 opens with what appears to be dispassionate information: 'I was three-and-twenty years of age'. Pip's birthday is a week past; he and Herbert have moved (a year ago) to the Temple, and are living by the river. These factual details seem documentary, but they constitute the barest notation of the primary axes of experience, time and place in their most personal forms: my age, and where I lived.

The second paragraph gives more of Pip's circumstances: his relation with the Pockets, now that he is grown; his 'inability to settle to anything'; his taste for reading. The account is proclaimed as literary: 'and everything with me was as I have brought it down to the close of the last preceding chapter' (Ch. 39, pp. 330–1). It is as if we are being invited to step into his book, and join the present moment.

Herbert is away, reinforcing Pip's 'dull sense of being alone'. His 'dispirited' mood seems to slow the pace of experience – an impression supported by the repetitive and laboured rhythms of his account: 'I was alone, and had a dull sense of being alone. Dispirited and anxious, long hoping that to-morrow or next week would clear my way, and long disappointed, I sadly missed the cheerful face and ready response of my friend' (Ch. 39, p. 311).

The next paragraph turns to the outer world, but the weather itself, 'wretched . . . stormy and wet, stormy and wet; and mud, mud, mud, deep in all the streets', seems infected with Pip's frustration and despondency. The adjectives, 'wretched', 'furious', 'gloomy' and 'violent', ostensibly describing physical conditions, convey human emotions. Clearly it is for Pip alone that 'the day just closed as I sat down to read had been the worst of all'. Nevertheless, it is Pip's outward circumstances that form the subject of the following, longer paragraph. The river, the wind, 'like discharges of cannon, or breaking of a sea', the darkness and 'the coal fires in barges on the river . . . carried away before the wind like red-hot splashes in the rain' are the exact details of the moment. But they also implicitly evoke an earlier scene in red and black – on the marshes, in Chapter 1, and again at the recapture of Magwitch in Chapter 5, where 'the ends of the torches were flung hissing into the water, and went out, as if it were all over with him' (Ch. 5, p. 71).

That unemphatic echo contextualises this moment, broadening its significance without blunting its immediacy. The next paragraph has a similar duality: an inner depth of symbolism coincides with the surface drama. Pip's literal reading constitutes a metatextual prompt towards interpretation: bell after bell literally strikes a warning note; the intrusive wind recalls past exposure and warns of impending chaos. Finally, caught in a sub-clause, comes the first sound of the approaching encounter – a muted echo of the signal of Joe's coming:

> I read with my watch upon the table, purposing to close my book at eleven o'clock. As I shut it, Saint Paul's, and all the many church-clocks

in the City – some leading, some accompanying, some following – struck that hour. The sound was curiously flawed by the wind; and I was listening, and thinking how the wind assailed and tore it, when I heard a footstep on the stair. (Ch. 39, p. 331)

This is Dickens the dramatist at his best.

It is the reading-lamp – approppriate to both the dramatic and the interpretive situation – that Pip takes to see who is there. The rush of his senses and mind together receiving and placing experience, reading the moment, is intensely allusive but elliptical. Despite the parallels we have noted, it is not Joe's visit that Pip thinks of, but something further back, something more sinister and mysterious. Troubling connections are suggested but not explained or justified. This is concentrated narrative, squeezed into the interstices of the drama, at a high pitch of psychological reconstruction:

What nervous folly made me start, and awfully connect it with the footstep of my dead sister, matters not. It was past in a moment, and I listened again, and heard the footstep stumble in coming on. (Ch. 39, p. 332)

Pip's narrative point of view (actually a listening post) is precisely located within the limitations of the moment – yet the scrupulous annotation of 'awful connection' reaches back into the past, and forwards in dread. Both Pip's circumscription of knowledge and the capacity for further apprehension – starting from what he can literally see and hear, but reaching into what he can 'read' or understand – will be vital to the coming encounter, first as it happens, and then in the retrospective view of the narrative.

Pip calls out, and direct speech asserts the primacy of the moment. Yet even here a symbolic resonance can be heard. The dramatic divisions of event and interpretation, protagonist and antagonist, outer and inner world, are marked but not secure throughout this encounter. The surrounding darkness and turbulence correspond to Pip's inner depths:

'There is someone down there, is there not?' I called out, looking down.
'Yes,' said a voice from the darkness beneath. (*ibid.*)

The sequence of experience, coming upon Pip in the shape of a stranger as a complete surprise, and yet somehow answering to old anxieties, is meticulously traced. The sense impression is momentary; registering its implications takes longer. Both processes can be suggested verbally in sentence rhythms – abrupt (as in Pip's challenge), or careful:

> I stood with my lamp held out over the stair-rail, and he came slowly within its light. It was a shaded lamp, to shine upon a book, and its circle of light was very contracted; so that he was in it for a mere instant, and then out of it. In the instant, I had seen a face that was strange to me, looking up with an incomprehensible air of being touched and pleased by the sight of me. (*ibid.*)

That pluperfect 'had seen' is precisely chosen for a moment already passed, inscribing in its tense a lost opportunity of further perception.

'Moving the lamp as the man moved': Pip notes, unmoved, the details of his visitor's physical appearance. Dress, age, physical type, signal a history of exposure, travel, hardship. But this cool distance of observation is compromised by an unexpected gesture: 'As he ascended the last stair or two, and the light of my lamp included us both, I saw, with a stupid kind of amazement, that he was holding out both his hands to me' (*ibid.*). The physical coupling in shared lamplight is ironically counterpointed to Pip's interpretive blindness. Pip reads the gesture as transgressing formality. In fact it exactly and ambivalently expresses both a history of mute generosity, and its underlying demands as well. In this context, Pip's polite, impersonal challenge is deeply ironic, and that is not lost on his visitor, who picks up his tone, and superimposes it on his own expansiveness:

> 'Pray what is your business?' I asked him.
> 'My business?' he repeated, pausing. 'Ah! Yes. I will explain my business, by your leave' (*ibid.*).

Two levels of understanding are established here, turning on the different values of the word 'business': at once outrageously remote and peculiarly apt to their concealed relationship, which has worked financially, but covertly expressed a deeper human exigency, here about to be exposed.

Another paragraph of narrative and commentary intervenes to reinforce our relationship with one of the two actors in this scene (Pip) while also exposing him to us through his judgements on the other: 'for I resented the sort of bright and gratified recognition that still shone in his face'(*ibid.*). In the following paragraph our attention is more closely focused on the stranger, as his 'wondering pleasure' is stressed, while he is opened further to view, taking off his coat and hat. When he again holds out both hands, it is as if to cut back to the earlier gesture, bypassing the diversion into Pip's sensibilities, and asserting his own distinct response to the encounter. What emerges now is his disappointment.

This emotion derives from 'expectations' long cherished, a relish stretching far back from this moment, but imagining a future too. It is, ironically, just as those hopes are thwarted in a disappointment that he will shortly *share* with the stranger, that Pip realises 'I knew him'. A curious exchange of consciousness takes place: 'I knew him before he gave me one of those aids, though a moment before, I had not been conscious of remotely suspecting his identity' (Ch. 39, pp. 333–4). Pip enacts his recognition by taking the outstretched hands – though the limits of his comprehension are still clear in the rejection of an embrace. Besides physical gestures, he uses verbal formulae to keep his visitor at a distance, expostulating (ironically), ' "Surely you must understand" '; but then, 'My attention was so attracted by the singularity of his fixed look at me, that the words died away on my tongue' (Ch. 39, p. 334).

Magwitch's 'fixed look' challenges the 'singularity' of Pip's point of view in this encounter, much as the recognition of his 'identity' (a term which could, disconcertingly, indicate absolute difference or absolute similarity) compromises Pip's 'self-posession'. Magwitch picks up and returns Pip's own coercive auxiliary verb, and its accompanying adverb, so strangely at war with the main verb: ' "What, surely, must I understand?" '. It is not this counter-claim, however, that takes effect, but the sight of tears in his eyes, which moves Pip to a further effort of understanding. He takes a glass to keep his guest company, and asks how he has been living. But he soon 'turned off to a point that had just come into my mind' and returns to 'business', attempting to repay the two pounds delivered for Magwitch by the man in the pub (Chapter 10). Magwitch's reception of this settlement of accounts is more emphatic than Pip's earlier repulse. 'Still watching' Pip, he asserts his own point of view; takes the notes, lays them together, folds, twists, and burns them – appropriately – 'at the lamp'.

This deliberately controlled and expository performance marks a shift in the direction and tone of the scene. Now Magwitch dictates the dramatic progress through his speech – elliptical and allusive, like that lesson in mime – while Pip's part is the paragraphs of unspoken introspection and comment which punctuate the dramatic text. The psychological balance of the two men is expressed in this shift of narrative control. Pip has become a mere spectator. Yet, paradoxically, his inwardness with us is greater in this function, as we 'read' the scene together with him, deciphering its clues, recognising their implications, responding. Magwitch's success excludes him from this process: 'In his heat and triumph, and in his knowledge that I had been nearly fainting, he did not remark on my reception of all this. It was the one grain of relief I had' (Ch. 39, p. 338). When Magwitch sees Pip's books 'mounting up, on their shelves, by hundreds', he looks forward to Pip's reading them to him, but for display, rather than communication: this is a different concept of 'reading' – ' "And if they're in foreign languages wot I don't understand, I shall be just as proud as if I did" ' (*ibid.*).

Pip's reading skills allow him to interpret like a detective or a semiotician Magwitch's clues to their joint 'business', but it is another level of understanding which opens the further significance of the scene to him. This apprehension has a primary quality connected with the immediacy of those 'natural symbols' at the start of the chapter. It reaches below the conscious intellect, touching on felt truths: a mysterious concept; yet Dickens finds a way of expressing this quite simply:

> I tried to collect my thoughts, but I was stunned. Throughout, I had seemed to myself to attend more to the wind and the rain than to him; even now, I could not separate his voice from those voices, though those were loud and his was silent. (Ch. 39, p. 339)

With that silence, and the need for the stranger to be sheltered and allowed to sleep, the dramatic storm gives way to the intensity of reflection in the concluding two pages of this chapter, and this volume, of the novel. Dickens had used a situation rather close to this in *David Copperfield*, when David found himself obliged to let Uriah Heep sleep in his London rooms. In that novel, the social transgression and physical proximity of the two heightens the violent tension between them, revealing a strain in David's character which comes uncomfortably close to what he loathes – embodied in Heep. Here in *Great Expectations* there is an advance on that perception. Certainly, Pip's first response to his visitor is horror, and dread softened slightly by pity; then comes 'suffocating' abhorrence, as their bonds are revealed, and the convict confides, ' "Look'ee here, Pip. I'm your second father" '. Only after Magwitch has gone to bed does Pip think of his 'wrecked' ambitions, of Satis House and Estella. But then, 'sharpest and deepest pain of all', comes the knowledge that it was for this he had deserted Joe.

This thought reaches beyond the dramatic situation into the heart of Pip's emotional and moral being. It demonstrates a depth of self-knowledge that, despite blame, constitutes an unboasted triumph in this moment of despair. Thus Pip's recognition of his past betrayal seems illogically but persuasively knit together with his careful attention to Magwitch now. We see the irony of redemption in the catastrophe of expectations; an unforeseen development of character growing out of extinguished anticipation, even though the scene ends in exhaustion:

> When I awoke, without having parted in my sleep with the perception of my wretchedness, the clocks of the Eastward churches were striking five, the candles were wasted out, the fire was dead, and the wind and rain intensified the thick black darkness. (Ch. 39, p. 342)

This darkness – the 'thick black darkness' far into the night, which is of course by so much the nearer dawn – dramatically, symbolically marks an extinction of old hopes. But it is also by inference a turning point, and so it proves, in the tone and line of the novel. From this comes a kind of opportunity, the renewed opportunity for development that comes out of recognition. This subtle and complex movement is supported both structurally and symbolically between Chapter 39 and the end of the novel. Although we have already considered many of the episodes that come after the return of Magwitch, it is worth recalling and regrouping them here in order to recognise their cumulative tone and structural force. In this third volume of the novel we find a reversion to earlier patterns, but with repetition modulating into different tonal inflections, amounting to a careful reversal of former values as the first truth is searched out; now 'recognition' is substituted for 'expectations'.

So Chapter 42 gives us Magwitch's history, recalling the introduction of Joe's story in Chapter 7, but differing significantly in tone. This is a deviation, not a new beginning. Yet Pip's earlier response, excused originally as a 'little interruption' (Chapter 7) and long since lost in London habits, can now be recalled to foreshadow what is to happen, at this 'second chance', with Pip's 'second father' – and what that is to mean too for his older relationship with dear Joe as well: 'I broke out crying and begging pardon, and hugged Joe round the neck: who dropped the poker to hug me, and to say, "Ever the best of friends; an't us, Pip? Don't cry, old chap!" ' (Ch. 7, p. 78).

This pattern of reversion and of unexpected renewal continues. In Chapter 44 Pip goes back – again – to Satis House, to confront Miss Havisham and Estella on the subject of his changed expectations. His visit is structurally aligned with his long courtship, but now he has come to acknowledge the defeat of his longings, and to redefine his feelings as love without hope: this is when he makes his most direct statement of love, and his most resigned.

Retreating to London, Pip is intercepted by Wemmick's warning, 'DON'T GO HOME'. So the displacement originally encouraged by Pip's expectations, when he left the forge to become a gentleman, comes full circle. Magwitch has come back and Pip finds he must leave his London home. The prolonged and unavailing project to engineer Magwitch's escape is in turn a strange reversal of Magwitch's old plans for Pip. Pip is now directing operations – by this time the relationship between them is not merely recognised but acknowledged. Leaving Magwitch, Pip reflects on it: 'Looking back at him, I thought of the first night of his return when our positions were reversed, and when I little supposed my heart could ever be as heavy and anxious at parting from him as it was now' (Ch. 46, p. 392).

The ghost at the theatre (Chapter 47) corresponds to this backward-looking movement with uncanny propriety, bringing Compeyson out of the past (where he first appeared in the churchyard as the embodiment of a fictional ghost) in the wake of Wopsle and in grim modification of the *Hamlet* motif, so apt to ghostly haunting, revenge and indeed to the further perception that 'the readiness is all': that mood of quiet acceptance required for conclusion to be reached.

Another quasi-archaeological interpolation comes with the tracing of Estella's origins (Chapters 48–51). Digging for her past, Pip finds it intermingled with his own. It is a delicately oblique narrative demonstration of his own recent assertion (Chapter 44, p. 378) that she is 'part of my existence, part of myself'.

The cost of such disinterment of the past is demonstrated dramatically in Chapter 49, with the destruction of Miss Havisham in the clearly symbolic flames of light, 'soaring at least as many feet above her head as she was high' (Ch. 49, p 414). Pip, too, suffers in this catastrophe. His hands, naturally, but also symbolically, are burnt. That, however, soon appears to be no more than a prelude to an even more dangerous encounter with a presence deep in Pip's past (Chapter 53): the demonic Orlick. Orlick's trap, torment, terrible confession and indeed his escape from the hellish lime kilns, seem to endorse a reading of this figure as a function of Pip's own psychic life, requiring to be given full expression even though this means transgressing the canons of narrative realism. This episode is more nightmare than plot. It is particularly interesting that Orlick, having summoned, assailed and almost killed Pip, escapes unscathed into the night after bringing into the light of direct speech those obscure crimes for which Pip had felt himself strangely responsible: the suffering and death of his sister. Orlick is a figure of vital, though destructive power: one – like Estella, perhaps – who cannot ever be written out of the narrative, because he cannot wholly be separated from Pip himself.

Miss Havisham dead, Orlick exorcised, it remains for Pip to endure the passing of Magwitch (Chapter 56). After this he suffers another 'darkness' of serious illness, and a further 'eclipse' in narrative terms as he goes into voluntary exile before he is ready to come to the conclusion.

The weariness concluding Chapter 39 and volume two of the novel is figured in 'thick black darkness': an image which also recalls the opening of *Great Expectations* and foreshadows its close. All three moments are marked by darkness. But the end has a distinctive quality, and one which corresponds to the metaphysical rhythms of the work, seeking truth rather than pursuing the historical cycle, reporting events. Instead of fright (as at first) or wretchedness (as in Chapter 39) this night brings its own 'tranquil light'. The narrative has Pip making his way from the forge to fulfil his resolution to visit and part from Satis House, so slowly that day passes before he comes to the place. Dickens's gentle sentence rhythms convey Pip's lingering pace, and the expanse of time this opens up for registration and reflection on what he sees. Balance and hypnotic repetition delay and amplify the movement of the prose. This accords with the narrative action: Pip's return to old haunts, and his meeting and recognition there of Estella, also returned; the plot itself is using repetition to permit amplification in their relationship. Put like this, the scene sounds stagey and contrived. But in reading, the effect of this circuitry is rather calming than emphatic, expansive than dictatorial. What Dickens achieves (in the second of his proposed endings for the novel) is a masterpiece of ambivalence: a poised and open end, substituting inexpectancy for expectations.

This tone and space for understanding is paced out through approach and response. The last three pages of the novel, dealing with the return to Satis House, deserve a full analysis, tracing the movement of phrases, sentences and paragraphs. They develop, pause and withdraw in a wave pattern, growing, breaking and retreating. Here the impulse of the moment meets the retrospective view of the narrator. Discovery and recovery fuse together. Patterns supervene over words: phrases repeated and elaborated; sentences exchanged. See how mutual is the rhythm of recognition between

Pip and Estella: as if the consciousness through which the scene is perceived exists somewhere beyond the divisive boundaries of individuality; Pip, Estella; then, now:

> The figure showed itself aware of me, as I advanced. It had been moving towards me, but it stood still. As I drew nearer, I saw it to be the figure of a woman. As I drew nearer yet, it was about to turn away, when it stopped, and let me come up with it. Then, it faltered as if much surprised, and uttered my name, and I cried out:
>   'Estella!'
>   'I am greatly changed. I wonder you know me.' (Ch. 59, p. 491)

There is a crescendo here from the distance of 'figure' to the form of 'a woman', the 'it' to a direct voice. The process of recognition *enacted* within Pip is viewed through *Estella's* movements. Her greeting is heard in his. The point of view and the voice of the text move from one to the other and back. The 'wonder' is equal, the naming mutual. And what Pip feels seems curiously depersonalised. It transcends the moment. His thoughts turn, without explanation, to another scene:

> The moon began to rise, and I thought of the placid look at the white ceiling, which had passed away. The moon began to rise, and I thought of the pressure on my hand when I had spoken the last words he had heard on earth.
>   Estella was the next to break the silence that ensued between us. (Ch. 59, p. 492)

This 'he' (Magwitch), like the earlier 'it' (the figure of Estella), has a kind of neutrality beyond the busy narrative encoding of names and personalities. To understand these pronouns, to perform our own act of recognition, we have to bring together, as Pip does, his love for Estella with his love for Magwitch, and to feel in this moment the pressure of silence beyond that of explanation. This syntactical discretion corresponds to an emotional acceptance. The capacity to use pronouns rather than naming names expresses Pip's deepest understanding, and it holds together the memory of failure (Magwitch's death) and the possibility of success (a happy ending with Estella).

Dickens draws on the resources of symbolism and setting to support the narrative coincidence of Pip's meeting Estella in the grounds of Satis House. But what really brings them together at this point is their common readiness to meet: the change in each that has uncovered what has never changed. And despite their quiet maturity, Pip and Estella's conversation still exhibits something of the challenge that characterises their close relationship. Each gives as good as they get. Will they continue, as Estella says, 'friends apart'? The concluding paragraph, a carefully balanced single sentence, leaves this possibility open, even in turning away from it:

> I took her hand in mine, and we went out of the ruined place; and, as the morning mists had risen long ago when I first left the forge, so, the evening mists were rising now, and in all the broad expanse of tranquil light they showed to me, I saw no shadow of another parting from her. (Ch. 59, p. 493)

CODA: THE SUPPRESSED ENDING

Before arriving at the carefully balanced solution discussed here, Dickens had proposed a more definitive conclusion, in which instead of the meeting at Satis House, Pip encounters Estella two years later on in London. Estella, having been widowed, is remarried. Pip, walking along Picadilly with little Pip, must seem to her to be settled too. There is thus no possibility of their being reunited. But the relationship between them is resolved, and the final sentence reads:

> I was very glad afterwards to have had the interview; for, in her face and in her voice, and in her touch, she gave me the assurance, that suffering had been stronger than Miss Havisham's teaching, and had given her a heart to understand what my heart used to be. (p. 496)

What is the effect of losing this, and substituting Chapter 59 as Dickens chose to do? A change of tone, certainly, away from elegy towards something less certain; for the published ending is poised between romantic promise and ironic threat. One of these possibilities offers a happy ending, equal and opposite to the elegiac first conclusion. Pip and Estella separated for ever, or united at last: either makes a good ending to the plot. But either also resolves what is only held open by the ambiguity of the published version: that is, the vital uncertainty of the relationship between Pip and Estella as it has persistently been realised through the narrative. The attraction, refusal, desire, deferral between them, the 'wonderful inconsistency' which asserts identity but recognises loss, is what preserves the integrity of each and the pattern of relationship at its most distinctive in the novel. Where the suppressed ending offers the consolation of closure, the one substituted resists conclusion.

Notes

HISTORICAL AND CULTURAL CONTEXT

1. See *Dickens's Working Notes for his Novels*, edited and with an Introduction and Notes by Harry Stone, pp. 317–18.
2. On Bakhtin, see David Lodge (ed.), *Modern Criticism and Theory: A reader*, Chapter 7 'Mikhail Bakhtin: From the prehistory of novelistic discourse', pp. 125–56.
3. John Forster, *The Life of Charles Dickens*, p. 356.

CRITICAL RECEPTION OF THE TEXT

1. Two anthologies are particularly useful in extracting the criticism noted here: *Charles Dickens*, edited by Stephen Wall (1970), and *The Dickens Critics*, edited by George H. Ford and Lauriat Lane, Jr. (1961).

PART II

1. See Forster, *op. cit.*, p. 356.
2. After writing this I came across the interesting technical discussion of the rhetoric of recognition in Terence Cave, *Recognitions: A Study in Poetics*.

Select Bibliography

WORKS BY CHARLES DICKENS
(Novels in Serial Publication)

Pickwick Papers	1836–7
Oliver Twist	1837–9
Nicholas Nickleby	1838–9
The Old Curiosity Shop	1840–1
Barnaby Rudge	1841
Martin Chuzzlewit	1843–4
Dombey and Son	1846–8
David Copperfield	1849–50
Bleak House	1852–3
Hard Times	1854
Little Dorrit	1855–7
A Tale of Two Cities	1859
Great Expectations	1859–60
Our Mutual Friend	1864–5
The Mystery of Edwin Drood	(unfinished) 1870

CRITICAL WORKS

Baumgarten, Murray, 'Calligraphy and code: Writing in *Great Expectations*', *Dickens Studies Annual*, 11, (1983), 61–72.

Brooks, Peter, *Reading for the Plot: Design and intention in narrative* (Oxford: Clarendon Press, 1984).

Select Bibliography

Brown, James M., *Dickens: Novelist in the market-place* (London: Macmillan, 1982).

Byrd, Max, 'Reading in *Great Expectations*', *PMLA*, 91 (1976), 259–65.

Cave, Terence, *Recognitions: A study in poetics* (Oxford: Claredon Press, 1988).

Collins, Philip (ed.) *Dickens and Crime* (London: Macmillan, 1962).

Collins, Philip (ed.) *Dickens and Education* (London: Macmillan, 1963).

Collins, Philip (ed.), *Dickens: The Critical Heritage* (London: Routledge and Kegan Paul, 1971).

Connor, Steven, *Charles Dickens* (Re-Reading Literature. Oxford: Blackwell, 1985).

Dallas, E. S., 'On *Great Expectations*' *The Times*, 17 October 1861, reprinted in Collins (ed.), *Dickens*, pp. 428–30.

Dickens Studies Annual: Essays on Victorian fiction, edited by Michael Timko, Fred Kaplan, Edward Guiliano (New York Press, 1983).

Flint, Kate, *Dickens* (Harvester New Readings. Hemel Hempstead: Harvester Wheatsheaf, 1986).

Flint, Kate (ed.), *The Victorian Novelist: Social problems and social change* (World and Word. London: Croom Helm, 1987).

Ford, George, *Dickens and his Readers: Aspects of novel criticism since 1836* (Princeton: Princeton University Press, 1955).

Ford, George H. and Lauriat Lane, Jr (eds), *The Dickens Critics* (Ithaca: Cornell University Press, 1961).

Forster, John, *The Life of Charles Dickens* (1872–4), reprinted in Gadshill Edition (London and New York: Chapman and Hall, 1904).

Foucault, Michel, 'What is an author?' (1969), reprinted in David Lodge, *Modern Criticism and Theory: A reader* (London: Longman, 1988) pp. 197–210.

Garis, Robert, *The Dickens Theatre: A reassessment of the novels* (Oxford: Clarendon Press, 1965).

Gilmour, Robin, *The Novel in the Victorian Age: A modern introduction* (London: Edward Arnold, 1986).

Gittings, Robert (ed.) *A Selection of the Letters of John Keats* (Oxford: Oxford University Press, 1970).

Golding, Robert, *Idiolects in Dickens: The major techniques and chronological development* (New York: St Martin's Press, 1985).

Gross, John and Gabriel Pearson (eds), *Dickens and the Twentieth Century* (London: Routledge and Kegan Paul, 1962).

Hardy, Barbara, *The Moral Art of Charles Dickens* (London: Athlone Press, 1970).

Hartog, Dirk Den, *Dickens and Romantic Psychology: The self in time in nineteenth-century literature* (London: Macmillan, 1987).

Horton, Susan R., *The Reader in the Dickens World: Style and response* (London: Macmillan, 1981).

House, Humphry, *The Dickens World* (Oxford: Oxford University Press, 1941).

Iser, Wolfgang, 'The reading process: A phenomenological approach' (1972), reprinted in David Lodge, *Modern Criticism and Theory: A reader* (London: Longman, 1988), pp. 212–28.

Jordan, John O. 'The medium of *Great Expectations*', *Dickens Studies Annual*, 11 (1983), pp. 73–88.

Lacan, Jacques, 'The insistence of the letter in the unconscious' (1957), reprinted in David Lodge, *Modern Criticism and Theory: A reader* (London: Longman, 1988), pp. 80–106.

Lawrence, D. H., *Letters*, selected by Richard Aldington with an introduction by Aldous Huxley (1950) reprinted (Harmondworth: Penguin, 1971).

Lodge, David, *Modern Criticism and Theory: A reader* (London: Longman, 1988).

Lucas, John, *The Melancholy Man: A study of Dickens's novels* (London: Methuen, 1970).

Martin, Graham, *Great Expectations* (Milton Keynes: Open University Publications, 1985).

Miller, J. Hillis, *Charles Dickens: The world of his novels* (Cambridge, Mass: Harvard University Press, 1958).

Newsom, Robert, 'The hero's shame', *Dickens Studies Annual*, 11 (1983), pp. 1–24.

Oliphant, Mrs, 'Sensational Novels', *Blackwood's Magazine* (May 1862), reprinted in Collins (ed.), *Dickens*, pp. 439–42.

Orwell, George, 'Charles Dickens', in *Inside the Whale* (1940), reprinted in Wall (ed.), *Charles Dickens*, pp. 297–313.

Schlicke, Paul, *Dickens and Popular Entertainment* (London: Allen and Unwin, 1985).

Shaw, George Bernard, Foreword to *Great Expectations* (1937), reprinted in Wall (ed.), *Charles Dickens*, pp. 284–97.

Slater, Michael, *Dickens and Women* (London: J. M. Dent, 1983).

Smith, Grahame, *Dickens, Money and Society* (Berkeley and Los Angeles: University of California Press, 1968).

Stoehr, Taylor, *Dickens: The dreamer's stance* (Ithaca: Cornell University Press, 1965).

Stone, Harry, *Dickens and the Invisible World: Fairy tales, fantasy and novel-making* (London: Macmillan, 1980).

Stone, Harry, (ed.), *Dickens's Working Notes for his Novels* (Chicago: University of Chicago Press, 1987).

Swinburne, Algernon Charles, *Charles Dickens* (1913), reprinted in Wall (ed.), *Charles Dickens*, pp. 250–3.

Tracy, Robert, 'Reading Dickens's writing', *Dickens Studies Annual*, 11, (1983), pp. 37–54.

Van Ghent, Dorothy, 'The Dickens world: a view from Todgers's', *Sewanee*

Review, LXVIII (1950), reprinted in Ford and Lane (eds), *The Dickens Critics*, pp. 231–22.

Wall, Stephen (ed.), *Charles Dickens* (Penguin Critical Anthologies. Harmondsworth: Penguin, 1970).

Welsh, Alexander, *The City of Dickens* (Cambridge, Mass.: Harvard University Press, 1986).

Wheeler, Michael, *English Fiction of the Victorian Period 1830–1890* (London: Longman, 1985).

Whipple, Edwin P., 'On *Great Expectations*', *Atlantic Monthly* (1861) reprinted in Collins (ed.), *Dickens*, pp. 430–3.

Wilson, Edmund, 'Dickens: The two Scrooges', in *The Wound and the Bow* (London: W. H. Allen, 1941).

Wilson, William A., 'The magic circle of genius: Dickens' translations of Shakespearian drama in *Great Expectations*', *Nineteenth Century Fiction*, 40.2 (1985), pp. 154–74.

Index